Blockchain Scalability and its Foundations in Distributed Systems

Vincent Gramoli

Blockchain Scalability and its Foundations in Distributed Systems

 Springer

Vincent Gramoli
EPFL
Lausanne, Switzerland

School of Computer Science
University of Sydney
Sydney, Australia

ISBN 978-3-031-12580-5   ISBN 978-3-031-12578-2   (eBook)
https://doi.org/10.1007/978-3-031-12578-2

This Springer imprint is published by the registered company Springer Nature Switzerland AG
The registered company address is: Gewerbestrasse 11, 6330 Cham, Switzerland

I dedicate this book to my wife, Klara, and my children, Zoé, Hugo and Roméo.

Preface

This book is primarily dedicated to *(i)* engineers who want to refine their distributed computing expertise and take informed design decisions that can impact the security and scalability of their blockchain systems and *(ii)* undergraduate (typically 2nd year) students with basic knowledge of mathematics (set and graph notations) as well as basic data structure knowledge (linked list).

The content of this book results from the material of the second year course *COMP2121 Distributed Systems and Network Principles* and the 3rd year course *COMP3221 Distributed Systems* taught between 2012 and 2022 at the University of Sydney in Australia and various seasonal schools and workshops taught at other industrial and academic institutions. I thus would like to acknowledge the students and engineers who took these courses and provided feedback that led to the current version of the material presented herein. This book can be used as a companion textbook for the Massively Open Online Course (MOOC) called "Blockchain Scalability and its Foundations in Distributed Systems" offered by Coursera in collaboration with the University of Sydney.

I am grateful to my colleagues Dahlia Malkhi, Michel Raynal, Sara Tucci and Jiangshan Yu for providing comments on earlier versions of this book and to Rachid Guerraoui for hosting me while I was writing parts of this book, EPFL has been an inspirational place to accomplish this task.

I wish to thank Liming Zhu for suggesting to do research on the blockchain topic. I am grateful to my colleagues Nathalie Bertrand, Christian Cachin, Shiping Chen, Sean Foley, Ralph Holz, Seth Gilbert, Rob van Glabbeek, Guillaume Jourjon, Igor Konnov, Marijana Lazić, Mikel Larrea, Cesare Pautasso, Alex Ponomarev, Paul Rimba, Mark Staples, Bernhard Scholz, An Binh Tran, Ingo Weber, Josef Widder and Xiwei Xu for our fruitful collaborations on the topic of blockchain.

Last but not least, this book would not have been possible without the members of the Concurrent Systems Research Group at the University of Sydney who worked on blockchain research including Pierre Civit, Tyler

Crain, Parinya Ekparinya, Christopher Natoli, Alejandro Ranchal Pedrosa, Gary Shapiro, Deepal Tennakoon, Michael Spain, Pierre Tholoniat, Gauthier Voron and Pouriya Zarbafian.

This book is in part supported by the Australian Research Council Future Fellowship funding scheme (project number 180100496) entitled "The Red Belly Blockchain".

Lausanne, Switzerland,   *Vincent Gramoli*
Sept. 2021

Contents

Chapter 1
Introduction

> Arguing that you don't care about the right to privacy because you have nothing to hide is no different than saying you don't care about free speech because you have nothing to say.
>
> *Edward Snowden*

V. Gramoli, *Blockchain Scalability and its Foundations in Distributed Systems*,
https://doi.org/10.1007/978-3-031-12578-2_1

As the loss of trust in institutions continues to accelerate, so does the growth of faith in blockchain technologies. Indeed, the blockchain technology promises to radically transform the way individuals and companies exchange digital assets, be they cryptocurrencies or data, without the need to trust an institution. In 2008, as people lost trust in financial institutions in the midst of the Global Financial Crisis, the blockchain technology became a popular tool for exchanging a virtual money, called cryptocurrency, without intermediaries. A decade later, people started losing trust in social media institutions and the sharing economy institutions at large due to scandals where centralized institutions benefited from their monopoly to manipulate users. As a result, the blockchain technology promises now to disintermediate any exchange of digital assets or "data" by enabling what is often called Web3.

In this booming context, it is not surprising to observe that blockchain expertise is the most sought skills on recruitment platforms, like LinkedIn. In fact, this unprecedented demand of blockchain skills is driven by the vital need for the society to retrieve control over the way its data are handled. Blockchain skills are incredibly diverse and building a secure blockchain system or evaluating the risks of using such a software for a particular use-case is difficult. It typically requires a team of experts able to understand *(i)* the guarantees that the underlying communication network offers to the blockchain software, *(ii)* the consistency offered by the distributed algorithms at play, *(iii)* the possible exploits against a given cryptographic scheme, *(iv)* whether the incentives in place lead the system to an ideal state that satisfies enough participants and *(v)* the semantic of the programming language used for writing the (smart) contracts that manage the data. Such a plural knowledge requires a deep understanding of fields as various as networking, distributed computing, cryptography, game theory and programming languages. This variety makes it nearly impossible to find a person who can claim themself as a blockchain expert.

Of course, this book does not aim at teaching all these fields but rather focuses solely on distributed computing and networking. In particular, this book focuses on the foundational concepts of distributed systems the blockchain technology builds upon. These concepts are rooted in influential research results that were discovered in the last half-century. They are, on purpose, not tied to a specific implementation, like Ethereum Geth v1.10.12, or a specific programming language, like Wasm, that tends to evolve rapidly under the influence of competing solutions. Rather than listing specific implementation details, this book offers a more holistic approach: In short, we consider a blockchain system as a distributed implementation of a linked list data structure, where participants, equiped with a public key cryptosystem, send, over the Internet network, signed transactions that get ordered in a consistent ledger despite the presence of malicious participants.

This book is also motivated by the growing amount of misconceptions around blockchain systems that are found at too many occasions over the Internet. On the one hand, the excitement around this technology led some startups to develop quantum-resilient solutions on top of non-secure blockchain platforms. On the other hand, the blogosphere has, over time, wrongly associated the notion of 'proof-of-work' to 'consensus' even though the former solves a different problem from the latter. As one can expect with technology advances, more so-called blockchain solutions are also drifting away from the intuitive blockchain notion, at times offering a replicated database that tolerates the crashes of a few replicas, at other times recording events without ordering them.

Blockchain is however not a panacea. Many companies have investigated ways to adopt blockchains to automate their infrastructure, hence speeding up processes involving partners. Despite its promises to automate exchanges between partners targeting possibly conflicting objectives in a secure environment, these companies have struggled to apply them in production. In these limitations lie unsolved problems, like *security* as the ability to guarantee the protection of some partner against the malicious activity of another or *scalability* as the ability to increase the number of partners without hampering the performance. This book will equip the reader with an in-depth understanding of the foundational concepts that are required to make a blockchain scalable without annihilating security.

To summarize, this book aims at shedding light on these security and scalability issues, and offering ways to limit their impact by describing foundational and recent research discoveries in the domain of distributed systems. Chapter 2 explains why consensus is needed for implementing the blockchain abstraction in a distributed system. Chapter 3 presents how classic blockchains aim at solving the consensus problem. Chapter 4 presents solutions to the consensus problem in different message passing models. Chapter 5 considers variants in the network model considered, which leads malicious participants to steal digital assets. Chapter 6 presents ideas to cope with the issues seen previously in order to make a blockchain, which tolerates Byzantine failures, scalable.

Chapter 2
Consensus in Blockchain

> Codes are a puzzle. A game, just like any other game.
>
> *Alan Turing*

© Springer Nature Switzerland AG 2022
V. Gramoli, *Blockchain Scalability and its Foundations in Distributed Systems*,
https://doi.org/10.1007/978-3-031-12578-2_2

In this chapter, we introduce the blockchain abstraction. We first present the history of blockchain and the key results that led to its invention. We then present the key elements that allow it to be used to transfer digital assets. We finally motivate the need for a set of distributed machines, referred to as nodes or processes, to agree upon the series of blocks that constitute the blockchain. This consensus will be described in more detail in Chapter 4.

2.1 A Brief History

Blockchain builds upon discoveries in different domains of computer science. In particular, it relies on the achievements of cryptographers, cypherpunks and distributed computer scientists around the world. Modern cryptography appeared in 1975 with the publication of the Data Encryption Standard (DES) [IBM75]. The notion of digital signature appeared a year later and Whitfield Diffie and Martin Hellman offered a protocol to exchange keys securely [DH76]. At the beginning of the 80's, David Chaum, an American computer scientist and cryptographer proposed the blind signatures as a form of electronic carbon copy for payment systems [Dav83]. This system offers auditability and privacy of payments. In 1989, David Chaum founds DigiCash Incorporated as an electronic money corporation that sold its assets to eCash.

This privacy idea is one of the main motivations behind the Cypherpunk movement that Eric Hughes, Timothy May and John Gilmore started in the 90's. They decided to meet on a regular basis in San Francisco to discuss ideas related to programming and cryptography and created the Cypherpunk mailing list. As more and more people joined their discussion group, this mailing list allowed them to reach out to a wider group of people exchanging ideas and discussing development. A famous manifesto that Eric Hughes published on this mailing list compares cash to a primary way of offering an anonymous payment system required to maintain the privacy of an open society.[1]

Advances in distributed computing contributed to discovering the building blocks of blockchain as it is known today. In 1992, Cynthia Dwork and Moni Naor required a user to compute a moderately complex crypto-puzzle before being able to access a resource in order to avoid abuse of resource usage [DN93]. The solution to this crypto-puzzle progressively led to the concept of *proof-of-work* that is presented today by machines in mainstream blockchain systems to demonstrate the workload they have computed. At the end of the 90's, the British cryptographer Adam Back proposes a hash-cash mint, a partial hash collision generator, on the cypherpunk mailing

---

[1] https://www.activism.net/cypherpunk/manifesto.html.

list.[2] The idea is to use partial hashes to be made arbitrarily expensive to compute, but to be verified instantaneously to detect double spending. In 2002, Adam Back published his "Hashcash" concept in a technical report [Bac02]. In 2004, Hal Finney extended the previous proof-of-work with the idea of reusability.[3] He offered a system allowing a server's integrity to be publicly verified by online users.

Digital money became a reality at the end of the 90's when Wei Dai sent a message on the cypherpunk mailing list, describing a system called "b-money". Similar to today's blockchains, this system allowed users to transfer money between accounts represented as public keys. In 2005, Nick Szabo proposed Bit Gold, the crypto-currency that applies a chain of hashes to guarantee immutability [Sza05]. It is in 2008 that the first protocol to transfer a cryptocurrency in a peer-to-peer fashion without the need for a central intermediary is authored by Satoshi Nakamoto [Nak08].

The corresponding Bitcoin protocol is released open source as the first blockchain in 2009. Several years later, another type of blockchain appeared that many commonly refer to as "Blockchain version 2.0": Vitalik Buterin describes Ethereum based on a generic crypto-puzzle and extends this notion of cryptocurrency by allowing users to upload not only transactions but also *smart contracts* [Sza97]—programs that can be invoked by other users. Gavin Wood proposed then a detailed description of Ethereum by publishing its Yellow Paper that kept evolving since then [Woo15]. In 2016, the Decentralized Autonomous Organisation (DAO) was proposed as a smart contract system uploaded to the Ethereum blockchain. This raised $150 million dollars but was hacked.

Since then, continuous efforts have been devoted to make blockchains more secure and their performance scalable. We will discuss some of these results in Chapter 6.

2.2 What is Blockchain?

A blockchain is a chain of blocks similar to the linked list data structure that is typically taught to undergraduate computer science students. While it is the goal for a blockchain to be a chain, it is often the case that the existing protocols fail to implement a perfect chain. Instead they often allow the chain to fork as we will explain in Chapter 5, this is why we consider here that the blockchain can be a directed acyclic graph. Figure 2.1 depicts a blockchain whose prefix is a linked list but that forks at the end.

---

[2] http://www.hashcash.org/papers/announce.txt.

[3] https://cryptome.org/rpow.htm.

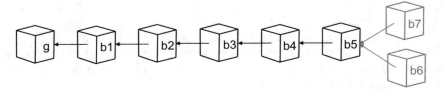

Fig. 2.1 The blockchain is a directed acyclic graph that can be viewed as a chain of blocks as long as it does not fork

2.2.1 The blockchain abstraction as a directed acyclic graph

Let the *blockchain* be a Directed Acyclic Graph (DAG) $\ell = \langle B, P \rangle$ such that blocks of B point to each other with pointers P and a special block $g \in B$, called the *genesis block*, which does not point to any block but serves as the common first block. What is interesting is that a new block gets appended to the chain by pointing towards the block that was appended to the chain last. More precisely, pointers P are recorded in a block as a hash of the previous block. For example, $\langle b_1, b_0 \rangle \in P$ is a pointer from a block b_1 to the block b_0 that was appended immediately before b_1: this means that block b_1 contains the result of a hash function applied to the content of block b_0.

This abstraction aims at offering a service to track ownership of digital assets. Consider a set of participants that act as users or *clients* and have an associated account, called *address*. These clients may send data to the blockchain abstraction to indicate how to transfer their assets to another address. These data can be of the form of simple transfers, or invocations of the function of a complex program, also known as *smart contract*, however, for the sake of simplicity we refer to all these requests as *transactions*. To transfer digital assets, a participant Alice simply creates a request comprising a signed transaction $\sigma_A(T_A)$ that is a representation of a transaction T_A that is signed by Alice's signature function σ_A. The transaction T_A contains the digital assets or *coins* that she wants to transfer and the recipient address to which she wants to transfer them. Hence the transaction request contains the signature, the assets and the recipient address.

2.2.2 Signed transactions

It could be the case that a malicious user, say Bob, would be tempted to try to steal the assets of Alice. In this case Bob would write a transaction T_A that transfers some of Alice's assets to his own address. To make sure that this request is not accepted by the service, each user keeps its own signature function private. Hence Bob can only issue a $\sigma_B(T_A)$ signed by his own signature function σ_B but cannot use Alice signature function σ_A. The system can detect that the request is not signed by the owner of the address from which the assets are withdrawn. As a result, the system considers this request as *invalid* and ignores it.

This is achieved using a public key cryptosystem: the transaction signature results from the user encrypting the transaction with its private key, the system verifies that the transaction is correctly signed by decrypting the signature with the public key of the owner of the address from which the assets are withdrawn. If the result of this decryption matches the transaction, then the signature is correct and the transaction can be recorded by the system, otherwise it is deemed invalid and the transaction is not recorded.

For a transaction to be *valid* it needs both to be correctly signed and to transfer assets that exist at the source address. The results of valid transactions are stored into the blocks of the blockchain either in the form of Unspent Transaction Output (UTXO) or in the form of balances, so that the blockchain and all its stored transaction results indicate what assets each user owns. It can be the case that two transactions *conflict* with each other when two concurrently issued transactions try to withdraw from the same account the same assets. For example, if two transactions withdraw 5 coins each from an account with a balance of 9 coins: both transactions cannot execute without violating the integrity of the corresponding account.

Unfortunately, the problem of maintaining asset ownership is not so simple because the blockchain is implemented in a distributed fashion. In particular, the blockchain abstraction is replicated at multiple nodes called *miners*, and users may perceive that the same asset is owned by different participants if they contact different miners.

2.2.3 Distributed implementation of the blockchain abstraction

The *blockchain system* often refers to the distributed protocol that implements the aforementioned blockchain abstraction. Due to its distributed nature and because it records asset transfers, the blockchain system is also commonly referred to as a distributed ledger. During the blockchain system execution, nodes generate new transactions and exchange them through the network. These transactions are grouped into blocks by special nodes, called *miners* and miners then propose blocks to other nodes. Miners try to agree on a unique block to append it to the chain. If they succeed, the current state of the blockchain indicates how digital assets have been transferred between accounts.

We consider a communication graph $G = \langle V, E \rangle$ with nodes or processes V connected to each other through fixed communication links E. (Notation $\langle v_1, ..., v_k \rangle$ of objects $v_1, ..., v_k$ represents a *tuple* of these objects.) Processes are part of a blockchain system S. Processes can act as clients by issuing transactions to the system and/or servers by *mining*, the action of trying to combine transactions into a block. For the sake of simplicity, we consider that each process possesses a single account (or *address*) and that a *transaction* issued by process p_i is a transfer of digital assets or *coins* from the account of the source process p_i to the account of a destination process $p_j \neq p_i$. Each transaction is uniquely identified and broadcast to all processes in a best-effort manner.

Algorithm 1 Blockchain construction at node p_i

1: $\ell_i = \langle B_i, P_i \rangle$, the local blockchain at node p_i is a directed acyclic
2:    graph of blocks B_i and pointers P_i

3: **Upon reception of blocks** $\langle B_j, P_j \rangle$:
4:    $B_i \leftarrow B_i \cup B_j$
5:    $P_i \leftarrow P_i \cup P_j$

Algorithm 2 describes the progressive construction of a blockchain at a particular node p_i upon reception of blocks from other nodes by simply aggregating the newly received blocks to the known blocks (lines 19–21). As every added block contains a hash (or digest) of a previous block that eventually leads back to the genesis block, each block is associated with a fixed index. By convention we consider the genesis block at index 0, and the blocks at j hops away from the genesis block as the blocks at index j. As an example, consider the simple blockchain $\ell_1 = \langle B_1, P_1 \rangle$ depicted in Figure 2.2(a) where $B_1 = \{g, b_1, b_3\}$ and $P_1 = \{\langle b_1, g \rangle, \langle b_3, b_1 \rangle\}$. (Notation $\{v_1, ..., v_k\}$ is used to denote a *set* of objects $v_1, ..., v_k$.) The genesis block g has index 0 and the block b_1 has index 1.

2.3 Double spending

This distributed nature of the blockchain implementation relies on the fact that different miners maintain their own replica of the blockchain, and these replicas typically diverge when some miners did not receive yet the data that others already received through the network. It is thus possible that the blockchain forks in which case distinct blocks are appended to the same block. This typically happens when each of two replicas append distinct blocks at the end of the same blockchain prefix. If the two branches contain transactions that consumes the same assets, then we call this a *double-spending*.

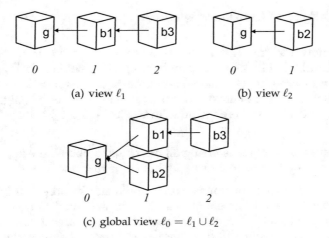

(a) view ℓ_1 (b) view ℓ_2

(c) global view $\ell_0 = \ell_1 \cup \ell_2$

Fig. 2.2 The first view ℓ_1 (Fig. 2.2(a)) and the second view ℓ_2 (Fig. 2.2(b)) diverge, leading to a fork ℓ_0 (Fig. 2.2(c)) where distinct blocks are at the same index of the chain

2.3.1 Forks as disagreements on the blocks at a given index

As depicted by views ℓ_1 and ℓ_2 in Figures 2.2(a) and 2.2(b), respectively, nodes may have a different views of the current state of the blockchain. In particular, it is possible for two miners p_1 and p_2 to create almost simultaneously two different blocks, say b_1 and b_2. If neither block b_1 nor b_2 was propagated early enough to nodes p_2 and p_1, respectively, then both blocks would point to the same previous block g as depicted in Figures 2.2(a) and 2.2(b). Because network delays are hard to predict as we will explain in Chapter 5, node p_1 may create the block b_3 without hearing about b_2. The two nodes p_1 and p_2 thus end up having two different local views of the same blockchain, denoted $\ell_1 = \langle B_1, P_1 \rangle$ and $\ell_2 = \langle \{g, b_2\}, \langle b_2, g \rangle \rangle$.

We refer to the *global view* as the directed acyclic graph $\ell_0 = \langle B_0, P_0 \rangle$ representing the union of these local blockchain views, denoted by $\ell_1 \cup \ell_2$ for short, as depicted in Figure 2.2, and more formally defined as follows:

$$\begin{cases} B_0 = \cup_{\forall i} B_i, \\ P_0 = \cup_{\forall i} P_i. \end{cases}$$

A *fork* is a set of multiple edges pointing towards the same block. For example, the global view ℓ_0 includes a fork as there exist two edges $\langle b_1, g \rangle \in P_0$ and $\langle b_2, g \rangle \in P_0$ that point to the same block destination g. Figure 2.2(c) depicts this fork.

2.3.2 From forks to double spending

Consider now that the DAG that represents the union of all blockchain views has multiple blocks at the same index k of the chain as in Figure 2.2(c). Let Bob and Carole be two merchants who sell real goods in exchange of coins and let Alice be a malicious user that issued two properly signed transactions T_A and T'_A that were included in blocks b_1 and b_2, respectively, such that:

- T_A consists of Alice transferring all her coins to Bob whereas
- T'_A consists of Alice transferring all her coins to Carole.

It is easy to see that both transactions should not be accepted by the system, because if Alice transfers all her coins to Bob she has no coins left to transfer to Carole, and vice versa. We say that these transactions *conflict* because they cumulatively withdraw more coins than what the balance would allow. However, because the transactions are accepted in different branches of the DAG, it is possible for Bob to observe that the transaction T_A has been included in a block, without seeing transaction T'_A, say because Bob did not receive block b_2. Similarly, it is possible for Carole to observe that the transaction T'_A has been included in a block, without seeing transaction T_A, say because Carole did not receive block b_1. If this fork situation is maintained for long enough so that Bob and Carole take an irreversible actions as a result of these transactions—for example, shipping the supposedly paid good—then we say that Alice has double spent: she has been successful at spending the same coins twice.

2.3.3 How to avoid forks?

To avoid forks, one must guarantee the uniqueness of a block at any index of the chain. This can be achieved by having nodes agree on this unique block, a problem referred to as the consensus problem [LSP82]. Put into the blockchain context, the consensus problem is for *nodes* (or processes) of a distributed system to agree on one block of transactions at a given index of a chain of blocks. This *consensus* problem can be more precisely stated along three properties: (*i*) agreement: no two correct processes decided different blocks; (*ii*) validity: the decided block is a block that was proposed by one process; (*iii*) termination: all correct processes eventually decide. A protocol solving the consensus problem, as will be presented in Chapter 4, is necessary to guarantee that blocks are totally ordered, hence preventing concurrently appended blocks from containing conflicting transactions.

2.4 Conclusion

Double spending is a problem that stems from the distributed nature of a blockchain system. It allows a malicious user to spend the same assets in two conflicting transactions. An easy way to achieve this is to create forks that will fool merchants. In order to avoid such a fork situation, we will have to solve consensus, hence guaranteeing that nodes agree on a unique block per index of the chain.

2.5 Bibliographic notes

Malicious behaviors are generally modeled by an arbitrary or Byzantine failure model that is named after the problem of generals attempting to reach an agreement in the presence of traitors defined by Pease, Shostak and Lamport [PSL80]. This failure model is detailed in Chapter 3. The uniqueness of the block avoids forks that could otherwise allow an attacker to double spend its coins in two branches [Ros12]. Consensus is known to be needed for a blockchain to remain a chain (without forking) [AKGN18, Ray18, ADPL+19] and for implementing a payment system if distinct nodes can issue conflicting transactions [GKM+19]. The UTXO model is the model used by Bitcoin [Nak08] that lists all unspent transaction outputs for each address whereby executing a transaction consists of consuming some UTXO and producing new ones. At any moment, the balance of an address can be retrieved by summing up all the UTXO of an address. The balance model as the one used by Ethereum [Woo15] does not use this notion of UTXO.

A way of achieving double spending consists of executing Finney's attack [Fin11] that consists of an attacker solo-mining a block with a transaction that sends coins to itself without broadcasting it before issuing a transaction that transfers the same coin to a merchant. When the goods are delivered in exchange of the coins, the attacker broadcasts its block to override the payment to the merchant. The vector76 attack [vec11] consists of an attacker solo-mining after block b_0 a new block b_1 containing a transaction to a merchant to purchase goods. Once another block b_1' is mined after b_0, the attacker quickly sends b_1 to the merchant for an external action to be taken. If b_1' is accepted by the system, the attacker can issue another transaction with the coins spent in the discarded block b_1.

2.6 Exercises

Question 1

Which of the following milestones marked the beginning of the history of blockchain?

a. Blind signature was proposed as a form of electronic carbon copy for payment systems
b. The Bitcoin protocol was written
c. Modern cryptography was made available to the public via the Data Encryption standard
d. The creation of the cypherpunk mailing list

Question 2

The cypherpunk mailing list was created:

a. Before the release of the Bitcoin paper
b. After the release of the Bitcoin paper

Question 3

Who originated the concept of "proof of work"?

a. Adam Back
b. Cynthia Dwork and Moni Naor
c. Hal Finney

Question 4

In 1998, Wei Dai sent a message on the cypherpunk mailing list, describing a system called "b-money". The system Dai described included a significant idea that is being used in blockchain systems today.

What was the significant idea first proposed in the "b-money" system?

a. Public keys to represent user accounts
b. Application of a chain of hash to guarantee immutability
c. A protocol to transfer cryptocurrency in a peer-to-peer fashion without the need of any intermediary

Question 5

When was the Bitcoin paper made available to the public?

a. 2008
b. 2013
c. 2018

Question 6

What was the name written on the Bitcoin paper:

a. Vitalik Buterin
b. Satoshi Nakamoto
c. Craig Wright

Question 7

Ethereum, the system first proposed by Vitalik Buterin, was commonly hailed as "Blockchain version 2.0". Although this system was based on crypto-puzzles, it was said to extend the notion of cryptocurrency.

How did Ethereum extend the concept of cryptocurrency?

a. Allows users to upload transactions
b. Allows users to upload smart contracts
c. Allows users to transfer cryptocurrency in a peer-to-peer fashion

References

ADPL+19.   Emmanuelle Anceaume, Antonella Del Pozzo, Romaric Ludinard, Maria
            Potop-Butucaru, and Sara Tucci-Piergiovanni. Blockchain abstract data type.
            In *Proceedings of the 31st ACM Symposium on Parallelism in Algorithms and Ar-
            chitectures (SPAA)*, pages 349–358, 2019.
AKGN18.   Antonio Fernández Anta, Kishori Konwar, Chryssis Georgiou, and Nicolas
            Nicolaou. Formalizing and implementing distributed ledger objects. *SIGACT
            News*, 49(2):58–76, jun 2018.
Bac02.   Adam Back. Hashcash - a denial of service counter-measure, 2002.
Dav83.   Chaum David. Blind signatures for untraceable payments. *Advances in Cryp-
            tology*, 1983.
DH76.   Whitfield Diffie and Martin Hellman. New directions in cryptography. *IEEE
            Transactions on Information Theory*, 22(6):644–654, 1976.
DN93.   Cynthia Dwork and Moni Naor. Pricing via processing or combatting junk
            mail. In *Advances in Cryptology (CRYPTO)*, volume 740 of *LNCS*. Springer,
            1993.
Fin11.   Hal Finney. Finney's attack, February 2011.
GKM+19.   Rachid Guerraoui, Petr Kuznetsov, Matteo Monti, Matej Pavlovič, and
            Dragos-Adrian Seredinschi. The consensus number of a cryptocurrency. In
            Proceedings of the 2019 ACM Symposium on Principles of Distributed Computing,
            pages 307–316, 2019.
IBM75.   IBM. Data encryption standard, 1975.
LSP82.   Leslie Lamport, Robert Shostak, and Marshall Pease. The byzantine generals
            problem. *ACM Trans. Program. Lang. Syst.*, 4(3):382–401, July 1982.
Nak08.   Satoshi Nakamoto. Bitcoin: a peer-to-peer electronic cash system, 2008. ht
            tp://www.bitcoin.org.
PSL80.   M. Pease, R. Shostak, and L. Lamport. Reaching agreement in the presence of
            faults. *J. ACM*, 27(2):228–234, April 1980.
Ray18.   Michel Raynal. *Fault-Tolerant Message-Passing Distributed Systems - An Algo-
            rithmic Approach*. Springer, 2018.
Ros12.   Meni Rosenfeld. Analysis of hashrate-based double-spending, 2012.
Sza97.   Nick Szabo. Formalizing and securing relationships on public networks,
            1997. http://szabo.best.vwh.net/formalize.html.
Sza05.   Nick Szabo. Bit gold, 2005.
vec11.   vector76. The vector76 attack, August 2011.
Woo15.   Gavin Wood. Ethereum: A secure decentralised generalised transaction
            ledger, 2015. Yellow paper.

Chapter 3
Blockchain Fundamentals

> I would be surprised if 10 years from now we're not using electronic currency in some way, now that we know a way to do it that won't inevitably get dumbed down when the trusted third party gets cold feet.
>
> *Satoshi Nakamoto*, 2009

© Springer Nature Switzerland AG 2022
V. Gramoli, *Blockchain Scalability and its Foundations in Distributed Systems*,
https://doi.org/10.1007/978-3-031-12578-2_3

3.1 Introduction

In this chapter, we study mainstream blockchain systems like Bit-coin [Nak08]. We look at how their proof-of-work mechanism can limit the power of the malicious nodes and how their consensus protocol copes with forks by pruning branches in order to converge to a unique chain of blocks. As we presented in Chapter 2, it is possible to exploit these forks to steal assets by double spending. It is thus important when building blockchains to think about all the actions that malicious participants could take to steal assets. This notion of malicious participant that can act arbitrarily has been called "Byzantine" in the distributed computing literature.

3.2 Failures and communication

The system comprises n nodes that are *asynchronous*, that is each node com-putes at its own speed. We consider the message passing model, where nodes communicate by sending and receiving messages. For simplicity we consider that nodes communicate through point-to-point reliable channel. This means that any pair of nodes is connected by a bidirectional channel so that upon delivery of a message, a node can identify the node that sent the message. Also, these channels are reliable in that they do not lose, create, duplicate or modify the messages. We will explain how to relax this assump-tion in Chapter 6. When not specified, we consider that the communication is asynchronous, that is there is no bound on the time it takes for a message to reach its destination but this time is finite.

In general a system *fails* if it cannot meet its promises and a distributed system of machines is typically a system that can fail if one of its machines fail.[1] Here we consider two types of failure models, the crash failure model in which up to f nodes can experience a crash failure or the Byzantine fail-ure model in which up to f nodes can experience a Byzantine failure. Each algorithm we will present will either work in one of these two failure mod-els or where no failures occur. More precisely, a node can experience only two types of failures:

- Crash failure: A node experiences a crash failure or fail by crashing if it halts but behaved correctly until it halts. Once a node has crashed, then it cannot do anything, it cannot even recover and send messages again with the same identity as before.
- Byzantine failure: A Byzantine node is a node that behaves arbitrarily: it can crash, fail to send or receive messages, send arbitrary messages, start in an arbitrary state, perform arbitrary state transitions, etc.

---

[1] http://lamport.azurewebsites.net/pubs/distributed-system.txt.

As an example, consider Figure 3.1 depicting two executions of the same node 0 as time increases from left to right. In the top execution, node 0 experiences a crash failure: it acts correctly until it halts. In the bottom execution, node 0 is Byzantine: it behaves arbitrarily by sending an arbitrary message, sending the same message multiple times and continuing its execution without halting.

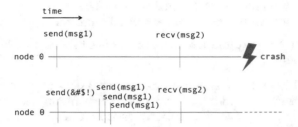

Fig. 3.1 A node experiencing a crash failure (top) during its execution follows the protocol until the crash occurs, after which the failed node stops acting. A node experiencing a Byzantine failure (bottom) can act arbitrarily by, for example, sending wrong messages, duplicating messages, while also sending and receiving some messages correctly.

We refer to a node that experiences a failure as a *faulty* node, and any nonfaulty node is a *correct* node. It is interesting to note that because Byzantine nodes can act arbitrarily, they can collude to make the system fail. Typically, by behaving arbitrarily Byzantine nodes can make more harm to the system than the crash nodes and they can even simulate crash nodes. So any algorithm that works in a Byzantine failure model, also works in the crash failure model.

Also, as each pair of nodes is connected by a channel, no Byzantine node can impersonate another node. Byzantine nodes can control the network by modifying the order in which messages are received, but they cannot postpone forever message receptions.

3.3 Properties of consensus

As mentioned before, the consensus problem has been an important research problem of distributed computing for the past fourty years. It finds applications in maintaining the consistency of a replicated state machine and helps totally ordering messages in a distributed system of machines.

Blockchain systems aim at solving the consensus problem, so that for a given index all correct nodes agree on a unique block of transactions at this index. As mentioned in Section 2 nodes may propose different blocks at the same index; this is generally observed with a fork. The classic definition of consensus is defined along three properties.

Definition 3.1 (Consensus). Assuming that each correct node proposes a value, each of them has to decide on a value in such a way that the following properties are satisfied.

1. Validity: any decided value is a proposed value.
2. Agreement: no two correct nodes decide differently.
3. Termination: every correct node eventually decides.

An algorithm has to fulfil these three properties to solve the Byzantine Consensus problem.

The validity and agreement properties are safety properties as they require the absence of anything wrong occurring in any execution whereas the termination is a liveness property as it requires that something good will eventually occurs in any execution.

3.4 Impossibility to solve consensus in asynchronous networks

It is important to note that consensus cannot be solved if the communication is asynchronous and there are failures [FLP85]. More precisely, there is no consensus algorithm ensuring both safety and liveness properties in fully asynchronous message-passing systems in which even a single node may crash. As the crash failure model is less severe than the Byzantine failure model, the consensus impossibility remains true if nodes may commit Byzantine failures. Although one might be tempted to try to design a protocol that does not always terminate but always guarantees the safety properties (validity and agreement) of consensus, this has recently been shown to be impossible as neither liveness nor safety can be ensured [CGG21]. To cope with this impossibility, various proposals relaxed the guarantees of the classic Byzantine consensus in favor of probabilistic guarantees by exploiting randomization, failure detectors or additional synchrony assumptions.

3.4.1 Failure detectors

To solve consensus, researchers have relied on failure detectors. In the crash-failure model, the weakest class of failure detectors that allows to solve the consensus is ◇S [CT96] that is equivalent to the eventual leader failure detector [CHT96]. Its eventual accuracy property guarantees that there is a time after which there is a non-faulty node that is never suspected by the non-faulty nodes. Building upon this guarantee, several consensus algorithms were proposed to solve consensus, namely, the nodes proceed in asynchronous rounds managed by a pre-determined leader or coordinator that tries to impose a value as the decision. Unfortunately, ◊S cannot be easily implemented in the Byzantine failure model.

3.4.2 Randomized consensus

Randomization can help solve consensus in the Byzantine failure model. Instead of terminating deterministically, randomized consensus algorithms terminate with a probability that tends to 1 as correct nodes take steps. Most randomized Byzantine consensus algorithms are binary in that the set of values that can be proposed is $\{0, 1\}$. Randomized Byzantine consensus algorithms typically use "local" coins—one coin per node—or a "common" coin—a shared coin that returns the same value at all nodes. This randomization is generally used to prevent Byzantine nodes from anticipating the value returned by the coin to force some correct nodes to diverge by adopting the opposite of this value. Randomized Byzantine consensus can either terminate with probability $(1 - \varepsilon)$ for some non-null but negligible ε or can be almost-surely terminating in that the probability of not terminating is asymptotically null. Probabilistic consensus makes some probabilistic assumptions, assuming for example that the scheduler is fair. This allows to solve consensus probabilistically without random coins as long as the number of Byzantine nodes among n nodes is $t < n/3$.

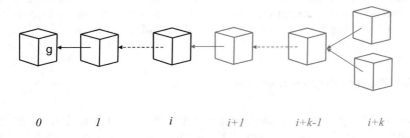

$$0 \qquad 1 \qquad i \qquad i{+}1 \qquad i{+}k{-}1 \qquad i{+}k$$

Fig. 3.2 A new block is decided at index $i > 0$ when the blockchain depth reaches $i + k$ (note that a blockchain of depth 0 is the genesis block)

3.4.3 Deterministic termination

Probabilistic termination is sometimes not enough. In fact, blockchain applications often need to be available, and thus need to be guaranteed to commit transactions. As an example, a financial application may require settlement finality, to reduce the risk of insolvency of a participant.[2] Blockchains, like Bitcoin-NG [EGSvR16], guarantee termination with some probability, hence leaving room for an application to be unresponsive in rare cases. Other consensus algorithms rely on some leader self-electing itself probabilistically [BPS16]. One can observe the creation of distinct blocks at the same index of a blockchain as a transient violation of agreement as depicted with the two blocks at index $i + k$ in Figure 3.2. Under the synchrony assumption, one can guarantee that in Bitcoin the block at index i is uniquely *decided* with high probability when the chain depth reaches $i + k$. Note that researchers already noted that this probability grows exponentially fast with k [GKL15]. And the recommendation of the Bitcoin project members is to use $k = 5$ or 6 confirmations in case the transfers are of "high" value.[3] (The value $k = 11$ or 12 confirmations was suggested for Ethereum by one of its inventors.[4])

To avoid being unresponsive, the application could decide of a timeout after which it considers the transaction successful even though the blockchain consensus did not acknowledge this success. For example, a merchant could wait for a predetermined period during which it observes any possible invalidation of the transaction by the blockchain. After this period and if no invalidation occurred, the transaction is considered valid. In the worst case scenario, the merchant may be wrong and the transaction may eventually be considered invalid, in which case the merchant will lose goods. Provided that this scenario occurs with a sufficiently small probability over all transactions, the merchant can predetermine its waiting period based on her expected gain over a long series of transactions.

3.4.4 Additional synchrony

The classic approach to solve consensus deterministically is thus to assume additional synchrony. Another way to solve consensus is to assume *synchronous communication* or synchrony, where every message gets delivered within a known period of time. This means that the algorithm can used this upper bound on the time it takes to deliver a message in order to work. In

---

[2] http://ec.europa.eu/finance/financial-markets/settlement/index_en.htm.

[3] https://bitcoin.org/en/you-need-to-know.

[4] https://ethereum.stackexchange.com/questions/183/how-should-i-handle-blockchain-forks-in-my-dapp/203.

particular, one could potentially use this bound to detect a failure if it does not get a response from a message it has sent two message delays ago. Another impossibility result indicates that consensus cannot be solved if $n/3$ or more nodes are Byzantine. This result applies even if synchrony is assumed as long as there is no authentication, meaning that the nodes cannot use signatures. But more generally this impossibility of solving consensus applies regardless of authentication with at least one Byzantine node in the asynchronous model.

Blockchain systems operate over a network, like the Internet, in which the assumption of communication synchrony is unrealistic. A more realistic assumption than synchrony is thus *partially synchronous communication* also referred to as partial or eventual synchrony. Communication is partially synchronous if after some finite Global Stabilization Time (GST), there is an upper bound Δ on message transfer delays. Note that, as opposed to the synchrony assumption, the bound cannot be used by an algorithm as it is unknown.

3.4.5 *Impossibility to solve consensus with too many failures*

Another impossibility result states that consensus cannot be solved among n nodes if the number of Byzantine failures f is greater or equal to $n/3$ even if we assume partial synchrony. One may think of using signatures as they are already implemented using public-key cryptosystem in blockchain systems as we have seen in Chapter 2. However, this would note help achieving a more resilient consensus protocol as in the partially synchronous setting with authentication we would need less than $n/3$ Byzantine failures anyway. Note that in the crash failure model, where we consider that f is an upper-bound on the number of crash failures and that there are no Byzantine failures, consensus is easier to solve. In particular, consensus in the crash failure model with partial synchrony can be solved among n nodes if the number of crash failures f is strictly lower than $n/2$.

3.5 Proof of work and mining

Miners have the role of creating blocks, by sometimes provably solving a hashcash crypto-puzzle [Bla02]. Given a global threshold and the block of largest index the miner knows, trying to solve a crypto-puzzle consists of repeatedly selecting a nonce and applying a pseudo-random function to this block and the selected nonce until a result lower than the threshold is obtained. Upon success the miner creates a block that contains the successful nonce as a proof-of-work as well as the hash of the previous block, hence fixing the index of the block, and broadcasts the block. As there is no known strategy to solve the crypto-puzzle, the miners simply keep testing whether randomly chosen numbers solve the crypto-puzzle. The mining power is thus expressed in the number of hashes the miner can test per second, or H/s for short. The *difficulty* of this crypto-puzzle, defined by the threshold, limits the rate at which new blocks can be generated by the network.

3.5.1 Proposing to the consensus

Miners initiate the consensus through a propose function depicted at lines 12–18 of Alg. 2 allowing them to propose new blocks after solving the cryptopuzzle (lines 12–18). Upon delivering blocks (lines 19–24), nodes decide upon new blocks at some given indices at line 24 depending on a function get-main-branch that is specific to the type of proof-of-work blockchain system in use (cf. Algorithms 3 and 4 for Bitcoin and Ethereum corresponding function, respectively). We refer to the computational power of a miner as its *mining power* and we denote the total mining power t as the sum of the mining powers of all miners in V. Each miner tries to group a set T of transactions it heard about into a block $b \supseteq T$ as long as the execution of transactions of T do not make the account balances negative. For the sake of simplicity in the presentation, the graph G is static meaning that no nodes can join and leave the system, however, nodes may fail as described in Section 3.2. We consider that the network is partially synchronous in that there is no known bound on the delay it takes for the message to be delivered.

3.5.2 Decided blocks and committed transactions

A blockchain system S must define when the block at an index is agreed upon. To this end, it has to define a point in its execution where a prefix of the main branch can be "reasonably" considered as persistent.[5] More precisely, there must exist a parameter m provided by S for an application to consider a block as *decided* and its transactions as *committed*. This parameter is typically $m_{bitcoin} = 5$ in Bitcoin (Alg. 3, line 25) and $m_{ethereum} = 11$ in Ethereum (Alg. 4, line 25). Note that these two choices do not lead to the same probability of success [GKW+16] and different numbers are suggested by different applications [NG16b].

---

[5] In theory, there cannot be consensus on a block at a particular index [FLP85], hence preventing persistence, however, applications have successfully used Ethereum to transfer digital assets based on parameter $m_{ethereum} = 11$ [NG16b].

Algorithm 2 The general proof-of-work blockchain consensus algorithm at node p_i

---

6: $\ell_i = \langle B_i, P_i \rangle$, the local blockchain at node p_i is a directed acyclic
7:      graph of blocks B_i and pointers P_i
8: b, a block record with fields:
9:      *parent*, the block preceding b in the chain, initially $\perp$
10:     *pow*, the proof-of-work nonce of b that solves the cryptopuzzle, initially $\perp$
11:     *children*, the successor blocks of b in the chain

12: propose()$_i$:
13:     **while** true **do**
14:         $nonce = $ local-random-coin()
15:         create block $b : b.parent = $ last-block(ℓ_i) and $b.pow = nonce$
16:         **if** solve-cryptopuzzle($nonce, b$) **then**
17:             broadcast($\langle \{b\}, \{\langle b, b.parent \rangle\} \rangle$)
18:             break()

19: **Upon delivery of** $\langle B_j, P_j \rangle$ **with valid** *pows* **at node** i:
20:     $B_i \leftarrow B_i \cup B_j$
21:     $P_i \leftarrow P_i \cup P_j$
22:     $\langle B_i', P_i' \rangle \leftarrow $ get-main-branch()
23:     **for** ($b_0 \in B_i'$) such that ($\exists b_1, ..., b_m \in B_i : \langle b_1, b_0 \rangle, \langle b_2, b_1 \rangle..., \langle b_m, b_{m-1} \rangle \in P_i$) **do**
24:         **if** b_0 is not yet decided **then** decide(b_0)

Definition 3.2 (Transaction commit). Let $\ell_i = \langle B_i, P_i \rangle$ be the blockchain view at node p_i in system S. For a transaction tx to be *locally committed* at p_i, the conjunction of the following properties must hold in p_i's view ℓ_i:

1. Transaction tx has to be in a block $b_0 \in B_i$ of the main branch of system S. Formally, $tx \in b_0 \wedge b_0 \in B_i' : c_i = \langle B_i', P_i' \rangle = $ get-main-branch()$_i$.
2. There should be a subsequence of m blocks $b_1, ..., b_m$ appended after block b. Formally, $\exists b_1, ..., b_m \in B_i : \langle b_1, b_0 \rangle, \langle b_2, b_1 \rangle, ..., \langle b_m, b_{m-1} \rangle \in P_i$. (In short, we say that b_0 is *decided*.)

A transaction tx is *committed* if there exists a correct node p_i where tx is *locally committed*.

Property (1) is needed because nodes eventually agree on the main branch that defines the current state of accounts in the system—blocks that are not part of the main branch are ignored. Property (2) is necessary to guarantee that the blocks and transactions currently in the main branch will persist and remain in the main branch. Before these additional blocks are created, nodes may not have reached consensus regarding the unique blocks b at index j in the chain. This is illustrated by the fork of Figure 2.2 where nodes consider, respectively, the pointer $\langle b_1, g \rangle$ and the pointer $\langle b_2, g \rangle$ in their local blockchain view. By waiting for m blocks were m is given by the blockchain system, the system guarantees with a reasonably high probability that nodes will agree on the same block b.

For example, consider a fictive blockchain system with $m_{fictive} = 2$ that selects the heaviest branch (Alg. 4, lines 27–34) as its main branch. If the blockchain state was the one depicted in Figure 3.3, then blocks b_2 and b_5 would be decided and all their transactions would be committed. This is because they are both part of the main branch and they are followed by at least 2 blocks, b_8 and b_{13}. (Note that we omit the genesis block as it is always considered decided but does not include any requested transaction.)

3.6 Resolving forks

To resolve the forks and define a deterministic state agreed upon by all nodes, a blockchain system must select a *main branch*, as a unique sequence of blocks, based on the tree. Building upon the general proof-of-work consensus algorithm (Alg. 2), we present now the characteristics of the Bitcoin consensus algorithm (Alg. 3) [Nak08] and also the GHOST [SZ15] protocol (Alg. 4) that inspired the design of Ethereum [Woo15].

The difficulty of the cryptopuzzles used in Bitcoin produces a block every 10 minutes in expectation. The advantage of this long period, is that it is relatively rare for the blockchain to fork because blocks are rarely mined during the time others are propagated to the rest of the nodes.

Algorithm 3 The additional field and functions used by the Nakamoto consensus algorithm at p_i

---

25: $m = 5$, the number of blocks to be appended after the block containing
26: $\quad tx$, for tx to be committed in Bitcoin

27: get-main-branch$()_i$:
28: $\quad b \leftarrow$ genesis-block(B_i)
29: $\quad$ **while** $b.children \neq \emptyset$ **do**
30: $\quad\quad block \leftarrow \text{argmax}_{c \in b.children}\{\text{depth}(c)\}$
31: $\quad\quad B \leftarrow B \cup \{block\}$
32: $\quad\quad P \leftarrow P \cup \{\langle block, b\rangle\}$
33: $\quad\quad b \leftarrow block$
34: $\quad$ **return** $\langle B, P\rangle$

35: depth$(b)_i$:
36: $\quad$ **if** $b.children = \emptyset$ **then return** 1
37: $\quad$ **else return** $1 + \max_{c \in b.children} \text{depth}(c)$

Algorithm 3 depicts the Bitcoin-specific pseudocode that includes its consensus protocol to decide on a particular block at some index (lines 27–37) and the choice of parameter m (line 25) explained in Section 3.5.2. When a fork occurs, the Bitcoin protocol resolves it by selecting the deepest branch as the main branch (lines 27–34) by iteratively selecting the root of the deepest subtree (line 30). When node p_i is done with this pruning, it obtains the main branch of its blockchain view. Note that the pseudocode for checking whether a block is decided and a transaction committed based on this parameter m is common to Bitcoin and Ethereum, and was presented in lines 19–24 of Alg. 2; only the parameter m used in these lines differs between the Bitcoin consensus algorithm (Alg. 3, line 25) and this variant of the Ethereum consensus algorithm (Alg. 4, line 25).

3.7 The 51% Attack

Double spending is not as simple as we discussed in Chapter 2 when the external action is taken after one of the two transactions is committed by the blockchain. Rosenfeld's attack [Ros12] consists of issuing a transaction to a merchant. The adversary then starts solo-mining a longer branch while waiting for m blocks to be appended so that the merchant takes an external action in response to the commit. The attack success probability depends on the adversary mining power and the number m of blocks the merchant waits before taking an external action. However, when the adversary has more mining power than the rest of the system, the attack, also called *majority hashrate attack* or *51-percent attack*, is expected to be successful, regardless of the value m. To make the attack successful when the adversary owns only a quarter of the mining power, the adversary can incentivize other miners to form a coalition [ES14] until the coalition owns more than half of the total mining power.

Without a quarter of the mining power, discarding a committed transaction in Bitcoin requires additional power, like the control over the network. It is well known that delaying network messages can impact Bitcoin [DW13, PSS16, SZ15, GKKT16, NKMS16]. Decker and Wattenhoffer already observed that Bitcoin suffered from block propagation delays [DW13]. Godel et al. [GKKT16] analyzed the effect of propagation delays on Bitcoin using a Markov process. Garay et al. [GKL15] investigated Bitcoin in the synchronous communication setting. Pass et al. [PSS16] extended the analysis for when the bound on message delivery is unknown and showed in their model that the difficulty of Bitcoin's crypto-difficulty has to be adapted depending on the bound on the communication delays. This series of work reveal an important limitation of Bitcoin: delaying propagation of blocks can waste the computational effort of correct nodes by letting them mine blocks unnecessarily at the same index of the chain. In this case, the adversary does not need more mining power than the correct miners, but simply needs to expand its local blockchain faster than the growth of the longest branch of the correct blockchain.

Although its implementation differs, Ethereum initially proposed to use a variant of the GHOST protocol to cope with this issue [SZ15]. The idea was

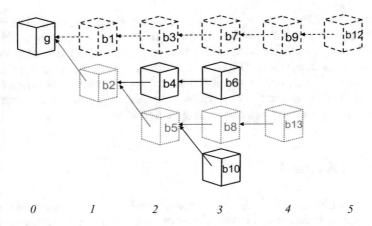

Fig. 3.3 Nakamoto's consensus protocol at the heart of Bitcoin selects the main branch as the deepest branch (in dashed lines) whereas the GHOST consensus protocol follows the heaviest subtree (in dotted lines)

simply to account for the blocks proposed by correct miners in the multiple branches of the correct blockchain to select the main branch. As a result, growing a branch the fastest is not sufficient for an adversary of Ethereum to be able to double spend.

Algorithm 4 The additional field and functions used by the GHOST consensus algorithm at p_i

---

25: $m = 11$, the number of blocks to be appended after the block containing
26:    tx, for tx to be committed in Ethereum (since Homestead v1.3.5)

27: get-main-branch$()_i$:
28:    $b \leftarrow$ genesis-block(B_i)
29:    **while** $b.children \neq \emptyset$ **do**
30:       $block \leftarrow \text{argmax}_{c \in b.children}\{\text{num-desc}(c)\}$
31:       $B \leftarrow B \cup \{block\}$
32:       $P \leftarrow P \cup \{\langle block, b\rangle\}$
33:       $b \leftarrow block$
34:    **return** $\langle B, P\rangle$.

35: num-desc$(b)_i$:
36:    **if** $b.children = \emptyset$ **then return** 1
37:    **else return** $1 + \sum_{c \in b.children} \text{num-desc}(c)$

3.8 The GHOST protocol

As opposed to the Bitcoin protocol, Ethereum generates one block every ~14 seconds. While it reduces latency and improves throughput (i.e., number of transactions committed per unit of time), it also favors transient forks as miners are more likely to propose new blocks without having heard yet about the latest mined blocks. To avoid wasting large mining efforts while resolving forks, Ethereum suggested to use a variant of the GHOST (Greedy Heaviest Observed Subtree) consensus algorithm that accounts for the so called *uncles* blocks of discarded branches. In contrast with the Bitcoin consensus protocol, the GHOST consensus protocol iteratively selects, as the successor block, the root of the subtree that contains the largest number of nodes (cf. Algorithm 4). Note that the current code of Ethereum selects a branch based on the difficulty of the cryptopuzzles solved to obtain the blocks of this branch without comparing the sizes of the subtrees.

The main difference between Nakamoto and the GHOST consensus protocol is depicted in Figure 3.3, where the dashed blocks represent the main branch selected by Nakamoto's consensus protocol and the dotted blocks represent the main branch selected by GHOST.

3.9 Conclusion

Mainstream blockchain systems like Bitcoin and Ethereum require miners to solve a crypto-puzzle whose solution gets included as a proof-of-work in a new block. These blockchains recover from forks by running a consensus protocol that eventually chooses one branch among multiple ones, based on its length, difficulty or weight. By acquiring more than half of the mining power, an adversary can still double spend, an attack called the 51% attack. The next chapter is dedicated to explaining how the literature on consensus algorithms can help remedy this problem by avoiding forks.

3.10 Bibliographic notes

The impossibility to solve consensus with $f \geq n/3$ failures is due to Pease, Shostak and Lamport [PSL80]. A didactic explanation is presented in [Ray18]. The impossibility to solve consensus in an asynchronous system when there is at least one failure is due to Fischer, Lynch and Patterson [FLP85]. The notion of partial synchrony and the impossibility of solving consensus with less than $f \geq n/3$ in the partially synchronous setting is due to Lynch, Dwork and Stockmeyer [DLS88].

The idea of randomized consensus based on a common coin is due to Rabin [Rab83] whereas the one based on local coins is due to Ben-Or [BO83]. Some recent algorithms converge in $O(n^{2.5})$ expected time when based on local coins [KS16] and in constant expected time when based on a common coin [MMR15a]. Randomized consensus algorithms are sometimes classified into $(1 - \varepsilon)$-terminating consensus algorithms that allow nodes to terminate with probability at least $(1 - \varepsilon)$ for some non-zero but negligible ε and almost-surely terminating consensus algorithms that ensure that the probability of the occurrence of a non-terminating execution is asymptotically zero, making the correct node terminate with probability 1 [BO83]. Note that consensus has also been solved probabilistically without using randomization and with $f < n/3$ of Byzantine nodes by making the probabilistic assumption of a fair scheduler [BT83]. Sometimes both a probabilistic assumption and randomization are needed to solve consensus [TG19]. Finally, asynchronous consensus was solved deterministically by assuming fairness [BGL$^+$22].

A replicated state machine shares similarity with blockchains [XPZ$^+$16] and some interesting differences have been outlined [CGLR18]. The 51% attack was presented by Rosenfeld [Ros12] as a situation where an adversary exploits more than half of the mining power of the system to create a longer branch that can override other transactions. The adversary issues a transaction to a merchant and starts solo-mining a longer branch while waiting for m blocks to be appended so that the merchant takes an external action in response to the commit. The attack success depends on the number m of blocks the merchant waits for and the adversary mining power. However, when the adversary has more mining power than the rest of the system, the attack, also called *majority hashrate attack*, is expected to be successful, regardless of the value m.

Algorithms 2, 3 and 4 were originally presented in [NG17]. It is unclear whether a transaction is "confirmed" after 1, 6, 12 or more block inclusions but the notion of *committed* transaction blocks was originally defined in [NG16b] as a transaction that would be followed by m blocks—this necessary number m of confirmations is generally provided by the authors of the blockchain system [Pro20, But15, But16a] but participants may choose their own parameter for security and speed. RepuCoin [YKDE19] aims precisely at coping against 51% attack by combining a proof-of-reputation with a proof-of-work. In Bitcoin [Nak08], a quarter of the mining power appears to be enough in theory to incentivize participants to join a coalition whose cumulative mining power will eventually reach strictly more than half of the total mining power [ES14], however, we are not aware of such an attack in practice. As we will see in Chapter 5, to attack blockchains without a significant mining power, researchers attacked the network.

3.11 Exercises

Question 1

Leslie Lamport once said "A distributed system is one in which the failure of a computer you didn't even know existed can render your own computer unusable". In the context of distributed computing, what does this quote indicate? Please choose the multiple possible correct answers.

a. A distributed system is a single system in a user's perspective
b. Computer support is essential for proper functioning
c. Your computer's functions are being controlled by an unknown other
d. Users are working in a system with multiple nodes that can impact on their experience

Question 2

What type of failure is the most serious?

a. Crash failure
b. Arbitrary failure

Question 3

Regarding crash failure, which of the following statements is correct?

a. It happens when a node can send wrong message
b. A node can send and receive a message before it halts
c. A node can interact as normal after it halts

Question 4

Regarding arbitrary (a.k.a. Byzantine) failure, which of the following statements is *not* correct?

a. Node can send messages that may be outside the domain specification
b. Node can flood the network with messages
c. Node can send or receive message according to normal patterns
d. Node behavior is predictable
e. Node can fake a crash failure

Question 5

True or false? If it never fails, a node is considered correct.

Question 6

Which consensus property is best described by the following statement? "Any decided value is a proposed value".

a. Termination
b. Agreement
c. Validity

Question 7

Which of the following statements best defines the property of termination?

a. The value decided in consensus cannot come out of thin air
b. Every correct node eventually decides
c. No two correct nodes would decide differently

Question 8

True or false? Consider the following distributed execution: This distributed

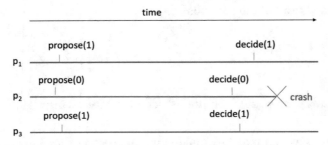

Fig. 3.4 A distributed execution with three processes

execution solves consensus.

Question 9

According to Fisher, Lynch and Patterson (1985), there is no solution to the consensus problem among n nodes if:

a. there is at least one failure
b. there is no failure
c. there is no assumption on the time it takes to deliver a message
d. there is an assumption on the speed it takes to deliver a message

Question 10

Which impossibility study shows that there is no solution to the consensus problem among n nodes if the number of Byzantine nodes is greater than or equal to a third of the nodes that are trying to solve consensus?

a. Fisher, Lynch and Patterson (1985)
b. Pease, Schostak and Lamport (1980)
c. Castro and Liskov (2002)

Question 11

According to Pease, Schostak and Lamport (1980), there is no solution to the consensus problem among n nodes if the number of _____ nodes is greater than or equal to a third of the entire set of nodes that are trying to solve consensus.

What kind of node failure are they referring to?

a. Byzantine
b. Crash
c. Any of these two types of node failure

Question 12

True or false? We can solve consensus if there is an unknown bound on the delay to deliver any message, we have 9 nodes participating in total: 6 correct nodes and 3 malicious nodes.

Question 13

True or false? We can solve consensus if there is no bound on the delay to deliver any message when we have 7 correct nodes and 2 malicious nodes.

Question 14

Which of the following attacks occur when a malicious Byzantine node creates fake, faulty nodes to the point where the number of faulty nodes exceed a third of the entire set of nodes?

a. Sybil attack
b. 51% attack
c. The Attack of the Clones

Question 15

Which of the following attacks occur when a malicious Byzantine node owns strictly more than half of the entire mining power of the system?

a. Sybil attack
b. 51% attack
c. The Attack of the Clones

Question 16

A malicious Byzantine miner mines until it has a branch longer than ones created by correct miners in the system. Eventually, as the particular system selects the longest branch, the Byzantine miner will have the ability to impose its blocks and the set of transactions it has chosen. The branch that contains blocks created by the correct miners will therefore be discarded.

Which of the following attacks is best described as above?

a. Sybil attack
b. 51% attack
c. The Attack of the Clones

Question 17

True or false? The solution to a cryptopuzzle is called the "proof of work". It is easy to find but hard to verify that it solves the puzzle.

Question 18

A cryptopuzzle is implemented when a miner is given a block and a threshold. A miner will then repeatedly select a nonce and apply a pseudo-random function to this this block and the selected nonce. How does the miner know when they have solved the cryptopuzzle?

a. They have obtained a result lower than the threshold
b. They have obtained a result higher than the threshold

Question 19

Multiple correct answers. A new transaction has been propagated and a miner has created a new block. Which of the following would a miner include in their newly created block?

a. Their private key
b. The solution to the cryptopuzzle
c. Some of the transactions the miner has received previously.

Question 20

In order to resolve a fork and maintain a single chain, which nodes in the network apply the strategy to choose the particular block that is at each index of the chain.

a. All the nodes
b. The nodes with the greatest computational powers
c. The miners

Question 21

The diagram below shows the potential of which of the following attacks?

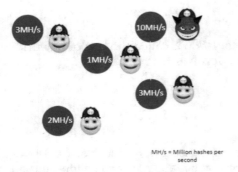

MH/s = Million hashes per
second

Fig. 3.5 A distributed system of correct and Byzantine miners with specific mining power expressed in millions of hashes per second

a. 51% attack
b. Sybil attack
c. The Attack of the Clones

Question 21

In the context of Rosenfeld's attack, what does a Byzantine miner need in order to override the blockchain and double-spend?

a. The lowest computational power within the network
b. A branch longer than the common branch

Question 22

True or false? In the context of propagation delay of blocks, a Byzantine miner must own more than half of the total mining power of the system for this attack to succeed.

Question 23

Which of the following problems related to selecting the longest branch does the GHOST protocol seek to address?

a. Sybil attack
b. Propagation delay of blocks
c. Rosenfeld's attack

Question 24

What does the "H" in the GHOST acronym stand for?

a. Heaviest
a. Highest

Question 25

How does the GHOST protocol resolve a fork?

a. Select the longest branch
b. Select the heaviest subtree from all the possible subtrees

Question 26

Ethereum (as well as the upcoming Ethereum 2.0) consensus is inspired by the GHOST protocol. However, GHOST is different from the existing Ethereum algorithm. What does GHOST take into account that Ethereum does not?

a. Depth of chain
b. Number of descendants for each block

References

BGL+22.   Nathalie Bertrand, Vincent Gramoli, Marijana Lazić, Igor Konnov, Pierre
          Tholoniat, and Josef Widder. Brief announcement: Holistic verification of
          blockchain consensus. In *Proceedings of the ACM Symposium on Distributed
          Computing (PODC)*, 2022.

Bla02.   Adam Black. Hashcash - a denial of service counter-measure. Technical re-
          port, Cypherspace, 2002. `http://www.hashcash.org/papers/hashca`
          `sh.pdf`.

BO83.   Michael Ben-Or. Another advantage of free choice (extended abstract): Com-
          pletely asynchronous agreement protocols. In *Proceedings of the Second Annual
          ACM Symposium on Principles of Distributed Computing*, PODC '83, pages 27–30,
          1983.

BPS16.   Iddo Bentov, Rafael Pass, and Elaine Shi. Snow white: Provably secure proofs
          of stake. Technical Report 919, IACR Cryptology ePrint Archive, 2016.

BT83.   Gabriel Bracha and Sam Toueg. Asynchronous consensus and byzantine pro-
          tocols in faulty environments. Technical Report TR83-559, Cornell University,
          1983.

But15.   Vitalik Buterin. On slow and fast block times, 9 2015.
          https://blog.ethereum.org/2015/09/14/on-slow-and-fast-block-times/.

But16.   Vitalik Buterin. How should I handle blockchain forks in my DApp?,
          1 2016. https://ethereum.stackexchange.com/questions/183/how-should-i-
          handle-blockchain-forks-in-my-dapp/203/#203.

CGG21.   Pierre Civit, Seth Gilbert, and Vincent Gramoli. Polygraph: Accountable
          byzantine agreement. In *Proceedings of the 41st IEEE International Conference
          on Distributed Computing Systems (ICDCS)*, pages 403–413, 2021.

CGLR18.   Tyler Crain, Vincent Gramoli, Mikel Larrea, and Michel Raynal. DBFT: Effi-
          cient leaderless byzantine consensus and its applications to blockchains. In
          *Proceedings of the 17th IEEE International Symposium on Network Computing and
          Applications (NCA'18)*, 2018.

CHT96.   Tushar Deepak Chandra, Vassos Hadzilacos, and Sam Toueg. The weakest
          failure detector for solving consensus. *J. ACM*, 43(4):685–722, July 1996.

CT96.   Tushar Deepak Chandra and Sam Toueg. Unreliable failure detectors for reli-
          able distributed systems. *J. ACM*, 43(2):225–267, 1996.

DLS88.   Cynthia Dwork, Nancy Lynch, and Larry Stockmeyer. Consensus in the pres-
          ence of partial synchrony. *J. ACM*, 35(2):288–323, April 1988.

DW13.   Christian Decker and Roger Wattenhofer. Information propagation in the bit-
          coin network. In *Proc. of the IEEE International Conference on Peer-to-Peer Com-
          puting*, pages 1–10, 2013.

EGSvR16. Ittay Eyal, Adem Efe Gencer, Emin Gün Sirer, and Robbert van Renesse.
          Bitcoin-NG: A scalable blockchain protocol. In *13th USENIX Symposium on
          Networked Systems Design and Implementation (NSDI)*, pages 45–59, 2016.

ES14.   Ittay Eyal and Emin Gün Sirer. Majority is not enough: Bitcoin mining is vul-
          nerable. In *Financial Cryptography and Data Security - 18th International Confer-
          ence, FC 2014, Christ Church, Barbados, March 3-7, 2014, Revised Selected Papers*,
          pages 436–454, 2014.

FLP85.   Michael J. Fischer, Nancy A. Lynch, and Michael S. Paterson. Impossibility of
          distributed consensus with one faulty process. *J. ACM*, 32(2):374–382, April
          1985.

GKKT16.   J. Göbel, H.P. Keeler, A.E. Krzesinski, and P.G. Taylor. Bitcoin blockchain dy-
          namics: The selfish-mine strategy in the presence of propagation delay. *Perfor-
          mance Evaluation*, Juy 2016.

GKL15.   Juan A. Garay, Aggelos Kiayias, and Nikos Leonardos. The bitcoin backbone
            protocol: Analysis and applications. In *Proceedings of the 34th Annual Interna-
            tional Conference on the Theory and Applications of Cryptographic Technique (EU-
            ROCRYPT)*, pages 281–310, 2015.

GKW$^+$16.   Arthur Gervais, Ghassan O. Karame, Karl Wüst, Vasileios Glykantzis, Hubert
            Ritzdorf, and Srdjan Capkun. On the security and performance of proof of
            work blockchains. In *Proceedings of the 2016 ACM SIGSAC Conference on Com-
            puter and Communications Security (CCS)*, pages 3–16, 2016.

KS16.   Valerie King and Jared Saia. Byzantine agreement in expected polynomial
            time. *J. ACM*, 63(2):13, 2016.

MMR15.   A. Mostéfaoui, H. Moumen, and M. Raynal. Signature-free asynchronous bi-
            nary byzantine consensus with $t < n/3$, $o(n^2)$ messages, and $o(1)$ expected
            time. *Journal of ACM*, 62(4), 2015.

Nak08.   Satoshi Nakamoto. Bitcoin: a peer-to-peer electronic cash system, 2008. `http:`
            `//www.bitcoin.org`.

NG16.   Christopher Natoli and Vincent Gramoli. The blockchain anomaly. In *Proceed-
            ings of the 15th IEEE International Symposium on Network Computing and Appli-
            cations (NCA'16)*, pages 310–317, Oct 2016.

NG17.   Christopher Natoli and Vincent Gramoli. The balance attack or why forkable
            blockchains are ill-suited for consortium. In *Proceedings of the 47th IEEE/IFIP
            International Conference on Dependable Systems and Networks (DSN'17)*, June
            2017.

NKMS16.   Kartik Nayak, Srijan Kumar, Andrew Miller, and Elaine Shi. Stubborn mining:
            Generalizing selfish mining and combining with an eclipse attack. In *IEEE Eu-
            ropean Symposium on Security and Privacy, EuroS&P 2016, Saarbrücken, Germany,
            March 21-24, 2016*, pages 305–320, 2016.

Pro20.   Bitcoin Project. Some things you need to know, 2020.
            https://bitcoin.org/en/you-need-to-know.

PSL80.   M. Pease, R. Shostak, and L. Lamport. Reaching agreement in the presence of
            faults. *J. ACM*, 27(2):228–234, April 1980.

PSS16.   Rafael Pass, Lior Seeman, and Abhi Shelat. Analysis of the blockchain protocol
            in asynchronous networks. Technical Report 454, Crytology ePrint Archive,
            2016.

Rab83.   Michael O. Rabin. Randomized byzantine generals. In *Proceedings of the 24th
            Annual Symposium on Foundations of Computer Science*, SFCS '83, pages 403–409,
            1983.

Ray18.   Michel Raynal. *Fault-Tolerant Message-Passing Distributed Systems - An Algo-
            rithmic Approach*. Springer, 2018.

Ros12.   Meni Rosenfeld. Analysis of hashrate-based double-spending, 2012.

SZ15.   Yonatan Sompolinsky and Aviv Zohar. Secure high-rate transaction process-
            ing in bitcoin. In *Financial Cryptography and Data Security - 19th International
            Conference, FC 2015, San Juan, Puerto Rico, January 26-30, 2015, Revised Selected
            Papers*, pages 507–527, 2015.

TG19.   Pierre Tholoniat and Vincent Gramoli. Formal verification of blockchain
            Byzantine fault tolerance. In *6th Workshop on Formal Reasoning in Distributed
            Algorithms (FRIDA'19)*, Oct 2019.

Woo15.   Gavin Wood. Ethereum: A secure decentralised generalised transaction
            ledger, 2015. Yellow paper.

XPZ$^+$16.   Xiwei Xu, Cesare Pautasso, Liming Zhu, Vincent Gramoli, Alexander Pono-
            marev, An Binh Tran, and Shiping Chen. The blockchain as a software con-
            nector. In *13th Working IEEE/IFIP Conference on Software Architecture, WICSA
            2016, Venice, Italy, April 5-8, 2016*, pages 182–191, 2016.

YKDE19.   J. Yu, D. Kozhaya, J. Decouchant, and P. Esteves-Verissimo. Repucoin: Your
            reputation is your power. *IEEE Transactions on Computers*, 68(8):1225–1237,
            2019.

Chapter 4
Consensus Fundamentals

> Part of the inhumanity of the computer is that, once it is competently programmed and working smoothly, it is completely honest.
>
> *Isaac Asimov*

© Springer Nature Switzerland AG 2022
V. Gramoli, *Blockchain Scalability and its Foundations in Distributed Systems*,
https://doi.org/10.1007/978-3-031-12578-2_4

In this chapter, we will show how to solve consensus. The consensus problem is a fundamental research problem of computer science that led to various proposals over the last four decades. We will study some of these proposals and learn about their tolerance to failures and their complexities.

4.1 Introduction

Today, with the recent advent of blockchains, various consensus implementations were proposed to make replicas reach an agreement on the order of blocks of transactions updating the distributed ledger. However, consensus has been known to be unsolvable in the general model since 1985 [FLP85]. While existing protocols were designed these past forty years to solve consensus under various assumptions, it remains unclear what are the guarantees offered by blockchain consensus algorithms and what are the necessary conditions for these guarantees to be satisfied. While the source code of most blockchain protocols is publicly available, the theoretical ramifications of the blockchain abstraction are rather informal. As main blockchain systems, like Bitcoin [Nak08] and Ethereum [Woo15], are now used to trade millions of US\$ every day[1], it has become crucial to precisely identify its theoretical ramifications to anticipate the situations where large volume of assets could be lost.

4.2 Consensus without failures

To simplify the presentation, let us first assume that no nodes fail and that the communication is synchronous. This way, all nodes can proceed synchronously, all executing the same line of the algorithm in parallel before proceeding to the next line, as if they were doing it at the same time. Recall that assuming synchrony actually means that each node can upper-bound the delay Δ it takes to transmit a message, hence guaranteeing that after sending a message, waiting Δ time is enough to guarantee that the receiving node delivers the message.

---

[1] https://coinmarketcap.com/exchanges/volume/24-hour/.

4.2.1 Consensus algorithm without failures and with synchrony

Algorithm 5 depicts an algorithm that solves consensus without failures and with synchrony. More precisely, function propose (lines 2–6) invoked by all nodes, that will decide the same value. The execution of the distributed algorithm simply consists of every node p_i broadcasting its initial value v_i to the other nodes at line 3. As a result of this sending, each node p_i then receives messages from other nodes p_j where $j \neq i$ at line 4. Finally, p_i stores these newly learned values in V at line 5 before deciding the minimum of these values at line 6.

Algorithm 5 A consensus algorithm executed at p_i that does not tolerate failures and assumes synchrony

---

1: V, the set of known values, it is initially set to $\{v_i\}$ the singleton containing the value proposed by p_i

2: propose$(v_i)_i$:
3:    send$(\{v \in V : p_i$ did not send v yet$\})$
4:    receive(S_j) from all $p_j, j \neq i$
5:    $V = V \cup S_j$ for all j
6:    decide$(\min(V))$

4.2.2 Correctness of the consensus algorithm without failures

This algorithm solves the consensus problem because it solves the three properties of the consensus problem we saw in Chapter 4. In particular, executing the function will eventually lead to line 6 where the node decides, hence guaranteeing termination. All nodes will decide the same value, because their set V will contain the values of all nodes as they are sent by all and received by all synchronously, which guarantees agreement. Finally, the minimum value guarantees that the value decided is one of the values of V that have been proposed by the nodes. Note that we pick the minimum among all values of V at line 6 while the algorithm could use another deterministic picking function, returning for example the median of these values V.

4.2.3 Complexities of the consensus algorithm without failures

The message complexity measures the number of messages that are sent during the algorithm. The message complexity of Algorithm 5 is quadratic because it simply consists of nodes exchanging messages in an all-to-all fashion. Hence we have n nodes sending one message to each of the other $n - 1$ nodes. This leads to $O(n^2)$ messages. Here we denote $f(x) = O(g(x))$ (resp. $f(x) = \Omega(g(x))$) if and only if there exists x_0 such that $f(x) \leq c \cdot g(x)$ (resp. $f(x) \geq c \cdot g(x)$) where $x \geq x_0$ and c is a strictly positive constant.

The communication complexity measures the number of bits that are sent during the algorithm. Note that the communication complexity differs from the message complexity when messages do not contain a constant number of bits. The communication complexity of Algorithm 5 is $O(b \cdot n^2)$ if we consider that the number of bits to encode each value is b.

The time complexity is the number of message delays necessary to terminate the algorithm. The time complexity is different from the message complexity when multiple messages are sent in parallel. As Algorithm 5 sends all messages in parallel, it only takes $O(1)$ message delays to terminate.

4.3 Consensus with crash failures

Consider now that there are f crash failures in that f nodes can fail by crashing, where $0 < f \leq n$. As before let assume that the communication is synchronous so that all nodes execute the same line of the algorithm before proceeding to the next line. The algorithm consists of executing a loop at lines 4–7 of $f + 1$ iterations, in each of which the nodes behave similarly to Aglorithm 5: they exchange at lines 5 and 6 the values that they have not exchanged yet and add to the set V all the values they know as their input value or as the values they received from other nodes at line 7. At the end of the loop, the node extract the minimum value among the obtained set V and decides this minimum value at line 8.

4.3.1 Correctness of the consensus algorithm with crash failures

In order to guarantee that Algorithm 6 solves consensus in the presence of f crash failures, we need to guarantee each of the three properties of the consensus problem: termination, agreement and validity.

Algorithm 6 A consensus algorithm executed at p_i that tolerates crash failures and assumes synchrony

---

1: V, the set of known values, it is initially set to $\{v_i\}$ the singleton containing the value proposed by p_i
2: f, the maximum number of nodes that can fail

3: propose$(v_i)_i$:
4:    **for** $k = 1$ to $f + 1$ **do**
5:       send$(\{v \in V : p_i$ did not send v yet$\})$
6:       receive(S_j) from all $p_j, j \neq i$
7:       $V = V \cup S_j$ for all j
8:    decide$\big(\min(V)\big)$

The protocol terminates by deciding after the bounded number $f + 1$ of iterations of the loop. Note that if $f = 1$ the algorithm resembles Algorithm 5, in which case it terminates after only one iteration.

Agreement is reached because at the end of the loop, every pair of nodes p_i and p_j have the same sets of values $V_i = V_j$ for any i and j, hence the minimum of these sets that are decided are identical. We know $V_i = V_j$ because no nodes can send a different value from the value v_i it initially had or from the values it received from others. In particular, no nodes can send different values to different nodes because they either fail by crashing in which case they do not send anything or they are correct. The worst thing a node that fails by crashing can do in this algorithm is to send a value to some nodes but to fail at line 5 before sending to all, hence some nodes receive its value and some nodes do not receive it. In this case, however, we are guaranteed to have an iteration of the loop where no new failure happens as the number of iterations is strictly larger than the number of failures f. In this particular iteration, all values partially sent by faulty nodes are re-exchanged so that all nodes receive them.

Validity is guaranteed because this set V_i contains only proposed values for any node p_i. Note that the algorithm also works when f is as large as n. In this case, it is easy to see that validity and termination are guaranteed for the same reasons as above. The agreement is also guaranteed because there is no two correct nodes that decide differently as there are no correct nodes.

4.3.2 Complexity of the consensus algorithm with crash failures

The message complexity is $O(n^2)$ in each iteration of the loop because each node sends messages to all other other $n - 1$ nodes. As there are $f + 1$ iterations of this loop, we obtain $O((f + 1)n^2)$ message complexity for the whole algorithm. Note that as f can be as large as n for this algorithm, this complexity is actually $O(n^3)$.

The communication complexity depends on the number of bits exchanged per message. Let b be the number of bits to encode the initial value of each node. As nodes exchange the values that they have not send yet, the messages can contain up to $(n-1)b$ bits. As we have $O((f+1)n^2)$ messages as mentioned above and each message is of size $O(bn)$, we obtain a communication complexity of $O(b(f+1)n^3)$ bits.

The time complexity follows from the number of iterations. There are $f+1$ iterations in the loop of this algorithm and in each of these iteration, messages can be exchanged in parallel. This leads to a time complexity of $O(f+1)$ message delays.

4.4 Consensus with Byzantine failures

We have only considered crash failures so far. Let us nows see how to solve the Byzantine consensus problem in order to cope with malicious behaviors that can be common in blockchain systems. To this end, we consider a simple model, where communication is synchronous in that every message is delivered within a known bounded time and that f is lower than $n/3$. We will see why relaxing the synchrony assumption in Chapter 5 and how to relax it in Chapter 6.

4.4.1 The problem of consensus with Byzantine failures

In order to find such a solution, we first need to refine our definition of the consensus problem in the presence of Byzantine failures. The previous definition of the consensus problem (Definition 3.1) is not well suited for the case where there are Byzantine failures. In particular, its validity property simply requires that the value decided is one of the proposed value, yet by definition a node experiencing a Byzantine failure can propose a value that is not desirable. Intuitively, we would like to avoid the consensus to output a value proposed exclusively by Byzantine nodes.

If we consider the *binary* Byzantine consensus problem, where the proposed and decided values are binary, i.e., they can either be 0 or 1, then one can change the validity property to require that the value decided is one of the values proposed by correct nodes. In this case, this new binary Byzantine consensus problem definition that inherits from the same agreement and termination properties as Definition 3.1, and replaces the validity property of Definition 3.1 by "the decided value is a value proposed by a correct node" could intuitively accept some solution. To illustrate what could be such a solution consider that $f < n/3$. To satisfy this new validity, it is sufficient to decide the value that was proposed $f + 1$ times. As there are f Byzantine processes, no values proposed exclusively by Byzantine processes can be proposed by $f + 1$ distinct processes. Note that this value is guaranteed to exist because there are at least $2f + 1$ correct nodes and each correct node can only propose one of two values, either 0 or 1. Definition 6.2 will introduce an even more general definition of the binary Byzantine consensus problem.

If we consider the *multivalue* Byzantine consensus problem, where there could be more than two distinct values that are proposed and decided, then there cannot be a solution that solves the agreement and termination properties of Definition 3.1 as well as the validity stating "the decided value is a value proposed by a correct node". With multiple values, there is no guarantee that there will be one proposed value that predominates sufficiently to be detected by any correct process. Typically, if there is no value proposed by more than f distinct nodes, then it is unclear which value is proposed exclusively by Byzantine nodes and which value is proposed by some correct process. We thus adopt a slightly stronger notion of validity than the one of Definition 3.1 by also requiring that in the case where all nodes are correct and they all propose the same value, then we have to decide this value. As the following definition of Byzantine Consensus (BC) finds solutions when there are more than two distinct values, it also finds solutions when the values are binary.

Definition 4.1 (Byzantine Consensus). Consider that each correct node proposes a value, the Byzantine consensus (BC) problem is for each of them to decide on a value in such a way that the following properties are satisfied:

- BC-Validity: Any decided value is a value proposed by some node and if all nodes are correct and they all propose the same value, then the correct nodes decide this value.
- Agreement: No two correct nodes decide differently.
- Termination: Every correct node eventually decides.

4.4.2 The EIG algorithm

We present the Exponential Information Gathering (EIG) algorithm that solves the Byzantine consensus problem (Def. 4.1). To understand the algorithm, each process maintains a tree structure, called an *EIG tree*, that has a degree n and a depth $f + 2$ spanning level 0, at the root, to level $f + 1$ at the leaf nodes. Initially, each process decorates its tree with the value it receives from other processes. If the value is not well formed, then the process uses label $\perp$ to indicate that the value is undefined. Otherwise it decorates the tree of the process with a label denoted $i_1, ..., i_k$ with value v to indicate that

i_k told i at round k that i_{k-1} told i_k at round $k-1$ that i_{k-2} told i_{k-1} at round $k-2$, ..., that i_1 told i_2 at round 1 that i_1's proposal is v.

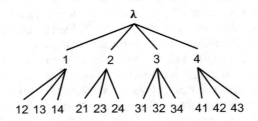

Fig. 4.1 The labels of the EIG tree at each process when $n = 4$.

For example, if $n = 4$ and $f = 1$, each process will build a tree whose labelling is depicted in Figure 4.1. If the tree node labelled 23 in the tree of p_1 (or process 1) is decorated with value 0 as it is depicted in Figure 4.2(b), then it indicates that process 3 informed process 1 that process 2 told him that its input value is 0.

At the end of the algorithm of $f + 1$ rounds, p_i updates the tree by traversing it bottom-up. It decorates each tree node with an additional *newval* as follows:

- For each leaf labeled x, $newval(x) = val(x)$;
- For each non-leaf tree node labeled x, $newval(x)$ is the *newval* held by a strict majority of the children of tree node x (or null if no such majority exists).

At the end, each process decides the value $newval(\lambda)$, which is the updated value at the root of the tree once the traversal completes.

4.4.3 *Example with $n = 4$ and $f = 1$*

To illustrate the algorithm, consider Figure 4.2 where $n = 4$ processes, namely p_1, p_2, p_3 and p_4, decorate their EIG tree as they exchange messages. We consider that we have $f = 1 < n/3$ processes that are Byzantine. Let p_3 be the Byzantine process and let 1, 1, 0 and 0 be the input values of p_1, p_2, p_3 and p_4, respectively. We are thus interested in the tree of processes p_1, p_2 and p_4 and how these correct processes reach a consensus despite p_3 lying to them.

All processes proceed in $f + 1$ synchronous rounds where they exchange messages. After the first exchange, p_1, p_2, p_4 received 1, 1, 0 from p_1, p_2, p_4, respectively. As p_3 is Byzantine, it sent 0 to p_1, and lied about its value by

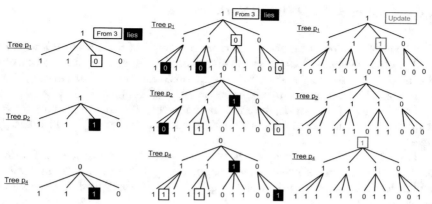

(a) During one commu-
nication round,
that p_3 is
p_1, p_2 and p_4
from p_1, p_2, p_3 and p_4, respectively. We can see that
p_3 lies to both p_2 and p_4.

(b) During a second com-
given munication round, p_3 lies to
Byzantine, p_1 and p_2 by saying that it
received received 0 from p_1 and lies
$\langle 1,1,0,0\rangle, \langle 1,1,1,0\rangle, \langle 1,1,1,0\rangle$ to p_4 by saying that it received 1 from p_4.

(c) At the end, each process
collects a *newval* at the root
of each subtree, by traversing from the bottom to the
top of the tree, in order to
decide the value *newval*(λ)
at the root of the tree.

Fig. 4.2 The EIG algorithm consists of all correct processes, say p_1, p_2 and p_4, building a tree such that the tree node 23 in the tree of process 1 is labelled with the value that process 3 told process 1 that it received from process 2. In Fig. 4.2(a) and 4.2(b), values from process p_3 are depicted within a rectangle and its lies are within black rectangles.. In Fig. 4.2(c), the updates are framed in grey.

sending 1 to both p_2 and p_4, even though its input value is 0. As a result, p_1, p_2, p_4 obtained the tree depicted in Figure 4.2(a). At the end of the fol-lowing round, correct processes p_1, p_2 and p_4 exchange what they received previously. The Byzantine process p_3 pretends that it received 0 from p_1 and from p_2 to process p_1 as indicated in the bottom left subtree of the p_1's tree, at the top of Figure 4.2(b). The Byzantine process p_3 also lies to p_2 by say-ing that it received 0 from p_1 as indicated in p_2's tree in the middle of Fig-ure 4.2(b) and to p_4 saying that it received 1 from p_4.

Finally, during the bottom-up traversal, each process identifies the pre-dominant values in the leaves of each subtree and sets the root of the corre-sponding subtree to this value. For example, in Figure 4.2(c), p_1's subtrees have all a majority of value 1 at their leaves, except the right-most subtree that has three 0 at its leaves, hence all subtrees have root value 1 except the right-most subtree that has root value 0. At the end they have all set their root value *newval*(λ) to 1 and decide this value as the outcome of the con-sensus.

4.4.4 Complexity of the EIG algorithm

To decorate the tree, one has to go from one level of the EIG to the next by exchanging messages. As the decoration requires to go from top to bottom, there are $f + 1$ exchanges to go through. As each exchange involves $O(n^2)$ messages, the message complexity becomes $O((f + 1)n^2)$ or simply $O(fn^2)$.

There are $f + 1$ rounds, in each of these rounds, messages can be exchanged in parallel. This leads to a time complexity of $O(f + 1)$ message delays.

The communication complexity is exponential in the number of failures because the content of previous messages is piggybacked in new messages, which leads to a communication complexity of $O(bn^{f+1})$ bits if each value is of size b bits.

4.5 Conclusion

The problem of consensus, although seemingly simple, is not easy to solve when the processes or participants can fail. In particular, we have seen three solutions offering different fault tolerance. The first algorithm is simple but solves consensus when there are no failures. The second algorithm is a variant that solves consensus when participants may fail by crashing but it takes longer to execute than the first algorithm. The third algorithm solves consensus when $f < n/3$ processes among n can fail arbitrarily, however, it requires to exchange a lot more information as its communication complexity is exponential. In all these solutions we assume that the communication was synchronous, we explain in Chapter 5 why this can lead to dramatic consequences when executing these algorithms over the Internet.

4.6 Bibliographic notes

The Exponential Information Gathering algorithm was originally proposed by Bar-Noy, Dolev, Dwork and Strong [BDDS92].

Designing Byzantine fault tolerant consensus algorithms is notoriously difficult. They are often large monolithic software [CL02], that are partially implemented [AGK+15a], and their complexity makes them subject to human errors [TG22]. The formal verification of blockchain consensus is an active area of research but, as far as we know, there is only one blockchain consensus algorithm that has been formally verified with model checking [BGL+22]. It will be presented in Chapter 6.

It is interesting to note that some blockchain technologies do not tolerate Byzantine failures [BCGH16, ABB+18]. This is the case of Hyperledger

Fabric [ABB$^+$18] or R3 Corda [BCGH16] that make the assumption that all the permissionned nodes that participate in the consensus trust each other. Although the version 0.6 of Hyperledger Fabric was originally designed to cope with arbitrary failures, we are not aware of any secure solution in production and a prototype Byzantine fault tolerant component [SBV18] does not make Hyperledger Fabric Byzantine fault tolerant [HSV$^+$22].

4.7 Exercises

Question 1

Let n be the number of nodes participating in a consensus algorithm. What is the message complexity of the consensus algorithm that works in the absence of failures as depicted in Algorithm 5?

a. $O(n)$
b. $O(n^2)$

Question 2

Let b be the number of bits needed to encode any value used in consensus algorithms. What is the communication complexity of the consensus algorithm that works in the absence of failures as depicted in Algorithm 5?

a. $O(bn)$
b. $O(bn^2)$

Question 3

What is the time complexity of the consensus algorithm that works in the absence of failures as depicted in Algorithm 5?

a. $O(1)$
b. $O(n)$

Question 4

Let f be the number of nodes that fail by crashing. What is the message complexity of the crash tolerant consensus algorithm as depicted in Algorithm 6?

a. $O(fn^2)$
b. $O(nf^2)$
c. $O(n^2)$
d. $O(f^2)$

Question 5

Can we reduce the bit complexity of the crash tolerant synchronous consensus algorithm as depicted in Algorithm 6?

Question 6

Let b be the number of bits needed to encode any value used in consensus algorithms. What is the communication complexity of the crash tolerant consensus algorithm as depicted in Algorithm 6?

a. $O(bfn^2)$
b. $O(b^2fn^2)$
c. $O(bfn^3)$

Question 7

What is the time complexity of the crash tolerant consensus algorithm as depicted in Algorithm 6?

a. $O(n)$
b. $O(f)$
c. $O(fn)$
d. $O(f+n)$

Question 8

What is the message complexity of the Exponential Information Gathering (EIG) Byzantine fault-tolerant consensus algorithm as depicted in Section 4.4.2?

a. $O(f+1)$
b. $O((f+1)^2)$
c. $O((f+1)n^2)$
d. $O(n^2)$

Question 9

Let b be the number of bits needed to encode any value used in consensus algorithms. What is the communication complexity, expressed in bits, of the Exponential Information Gathering (EIG) Byzantine fault tolerant algorithm as depicted in Section 4.4.2?

a. $O(bn(f + 1))$
b. $O(b(f + 1)^n)$
c. $O(bn^{f+1})$
d. $O(bn^2)$

Question 10

What is the time complexity of the Exponential Information Gathering (EIG) Byzantine fault tolerant algorithm as depicted in Section 4.4.2?

a. $O(f + 1)$
b. $O((f + 1)n^2)$
c. $O(f + n)$
d. $O(n^2)$

Question 11

True or false. One cannot solve consensus with synchrony (and without authentication) if $n = 9$ and $f = 3$.

Question 12

True or false. One cannot solve consensus with synchrony (and without authentication) if $n = 7$ and $f = 2$.

Question 13

What is the number n of nodes that should run a consensus algorithm to tolerate f Byzantine nodes in a synchronous network (without authentication)?

a. $f + 1$
b. $2f + 1$
c. $3f + 1$

Question 14

True or false. One cannot solve consensus with synchrony (and without authentication) if $n = 100$ and $f = 30$.

Question 15

Given that the bandwidth is a limited resource, which communication complexity would allow a consensus algorithm to scale better:

a. $O(bn^{f+1})$
b. $O(bfn^3)$
c. $O(bn^2)$

Question 16

What does it indicate about the three algorithms we have seen?

a. The solutions to the consensus in the presence or absence of failures have the same communication cost
b. The cost of solving consensus while tolerating failures depends on the severity of the type of failures
c. Solving consensus that tolerates arbitrary failures involves as much effort as solving consensus that tolerates crash failures

Question 17

What does EIG mean?

a. Exponentially incremental gathering
b. Exponential information gathering

Question 18

Why is the bit complexity of EIG increasing particularly fast with the number of participants compared to the other algorithm?

a. Mainly because one participant needs to send messages to all participants.

b. Mainly because participants relay the information they received previously.

References

ABB⁺18. Elli Androulaki, Artem Barger, Vita Bortnikov, Christian Cachin, Konstantinos Christidis, Angelo De Caro, David Enyeart, Christopher Ferris, Gennady Laventman, Yacov Manevich, Srinivasan Muralidharan, Chet Murthy, Binh Nguyen, Manish Sethi, Gari Singh, Keith Smith, Alessandro Sorniotti, Chrysoula Stathakopoulou, Marko Vukolić, Sharon Weed Cocco, and Jason Yellick. Hyperledger fabric: A distributed operating system for permissioned blockchains. In *Proceedings of the Thirteenth EuroSys Conference*, EuroSys '18, pages 30:1–30:15, 2018.

AGK⁺15. Pierre-Louis Aublin, Rachid Guerraoui, Nikola Knežević, Vivien Quéma, and Marko Vukolić. The next 700 BFT protocols. *ACM Trans. Comput. Syst.*, 32(4):12:1–12:45, January 2015.

BCGH16. Richard Gendal Brown, James Carlyle, Ian Grigg, and Mike Hearn. Corda: An introduction, 2016.

BDDS92. Amotz Bar-Noy, Danny Dolev, Cynthia Dwork, and H. Raymond Strong. Shifting gears: Changing algorithms on the fly to expedite byzantine agreement. *Inf. Comput.*, 97(2):205–233, 1992.

BGL⁺22. Nathalie Bertrand, Vincent Gramoli, Marijana Lazić, Igor Konnov, Pierre Tholoniat, and Josef Widder. Brief announcement: Holistic verification of blockchain consensus. In *Proceedings of the ACM Symposium on Distributed Computing (PODC)*, 2022.

CL02. Miguel Castro and Barbara Liskov. Practical byzantine fault tolerance and proactive recovery. *ACM Trans. Comput. Syst.*, 20(4):398–461, 2002.

FLP85. Michael J. Fischer, Nancy A. Lynch, and Michael S. Paterson. Impossibility of distributed consensus with one faulty process. *J. ACM*, 32(2):374–382, April 1985.

HSV⁺22. David Hyland, Joao Sousa, Gauthier Voron, Alysson Bessani, and Vincent Gramoli. Ten myths about blockchain consensus. In *Blockchains - A Handbook on Fundamentals, Platforms and Applications*. Springer, 2022.

Nak08. Satoshi Nakamoto. Bitcoin: a peer-to-peer electronic cash system, 2008. `http://www.bitcoin.org`.

SBV18. Joao Sousa, Alysson Bessani, and Marko Vukolić. A byzantine fault-tolerant ordering service for the hyperledger fabric blockchain platform. In *2018 48th Annual IEEE/IFIP International Conference on Dependable Systems and Networks (DSN)*, pages 51–58, June 2018.

TG22. Pierre Tholoniat and Vincent Gramoli. Formal verification of blockchain byzantine fault tolerance. In *Handbook on Blockchain*. Springer Nature, 2022.

Woo15. Gavin Wood. Ethereum: A secure decentralised generalised transaction ledger, 2015. Yellow paper.

Chapter 5
Making Blockchains Secure

> Although the [consensus] result is
> indeed correct, we have seen
> equally plausible "proof" of
> invalid results.
>
> *Leslie Lamport*

© Springer Nature Switzerland AG 2022
V. Gramoli, *Blockchain Scalability and its Foundations in Distributed Systems*,
https://doi.org/10.1007/978-3-031-12578-2_5

5.1 Introduction

In this chapter, we tackle the problem of security. As blockchain found applications to track ownership of digital assets, it is crucial for companies to adopt more secure blockchains than the ones proven vulnerable to network attacks before moving them in production.

We mentioned in Chapter 2 that a blockchain should prevent an attacker from double spending and we saw in Chapter 3 that violating consensus could lead to double spending but typically requires the attacker to own a large mining power, an attack which is very hard in a sufficiently large system.

We now explain, how one can double spend without owning a large portion of the mining power. In particular, we explain how a malicious user could violate the assumptions on which the previous consensus algorithms build and we describe the dramatic consequences such attacks could have. More specifically, we question whether the synchrony assumption is realistic and what an attacker needs to do to violate it. We then present attacks against mainstream blockchain systems that introduce and exploit network delays to double spend.

These attacks reveal an inherent lack of incentives for blockchain participants to act correctly. We thus discuss the need to hold participants accountable for their actions and discuss some directions to guarantee that participants are better off not misbehaving.

5.2 Beyond synchrony

The consensus algorithms we presented so far require synchrony, i.e., all messages must be transmitted in a known bounded time, say Δ. This synchrony assumption is convenient. For simplicity consider that the time it takes to do any local computation is negligible when compared to the time needed to exchange a message. It allows to know that a failure occurs if the message we expected in response to our message has not been received in 2Δ times.

In the context of blockchain, this synchrony assumption allows Bitcoin and Ethereum to know whether a transaction is committed. Consider that a block for index m of the chain is created at time at most t—say for example that p_i learns about the existence of this block at time t. Synchrony guarantees us that any reliable participant becomes aware of this block at the latest at time $t + \Delta$. As a result, all miners start mining a new block for index $\ell > m$ at time $t + \Delta$ and no new competing blocks will be proposed by correct miners for index m. At time $t + 2\Delta$, p_i is guaranteed to know the blocks proposed by the correct processes at index m. Provided that Byzantine miners do not have a sufficient mining power one can use this information to know which block at index m is part of the longest branch and hence identify, as depicted in Figure 3.2, the transactions that are committed.

Unfortunately, synchrony is unrealistic in practice as the time to transmit a message depends on the size of the message, the route that the message takes, the congestion of the network and other environmental factors that cannot be predicted. In 2004, the Computer Emergency Response Team Co-ordination Center at Carnegie Mellon University that collected computer security incidents in the US stopped doing so by arguing that attacks became commonplace. In 2017, typhoons damaged an undersea cable connecting Sydney to Hong Kong, which translated into a drop in quality of Internet connections in Australia. Human misconfigurations of the routing tables used by the Border Gateway Protocol to route traffic on the Internet often impacts messages delays over the Internet. So when malicious behaviors do not occur, either disasters or mistakes provoke unexpected message delays.

This problem is well-known and can be found in the eight fallacies of network and distributed systems. In particular, the network is reliable, the latency is zero, the bandwidth is infinite, the topology of the network does not change, the transport cost is zero and the network is homogeneous are well-known fallacies that are commonly assumed.

5.3 The Balance Attack

In the *Balance Attack* [NG16a], an attacker transiently disrupts communications between subgroups of Ethereum miners of similar mining power. During this time, the attacker issues transactions in one subgroup, say the *transaction subgroup*, and mines blocks in another subgroup, say the *block subgroup*, up to the point where the tree of the block subgroup outweighs, with high probability, the tree of the transaction subgroup.

Figure 5.1 depicts two blockchain views observed by two subgroups of the participating nodes. To double spend the attacker A sends a transaction in the bottom subgroup; consider that this transaction is included in block b_7. We refer to this bottom subgroup as the transaction T_A subgroup whereas we refer to the other one, the top subgroup, as the block subgroup. As the two subgroups have similar mining power, their blockchain views are expected to have similar weights and depths. It results that the attacker simply has to append few blocks to one of the two blockchain views to influence the decision regarding the view the system will eventually adopt. This is achieved by mining block b_6 in the block subgroup. When the subgroups start exchanging messages again, they both discard the bottom view as it does not contain the branch of largest weight or depth. The attacker can then re-spend the assets spent in T_A to complete the double spending.

Another option to achieve double spending in a similar situation would be to isolate a subgroup of smaller mining power than another subgroup,

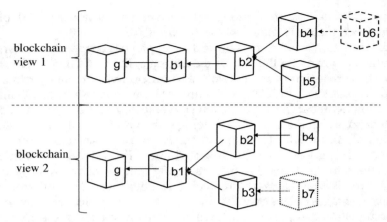

Fig. 5.1 The Balance Attack consists of an attacker isolating two subgroups of nodes, one to which it sends a transaction, another to which it contributes blocks

however, it would make the attack only possible if the recipients of the transactions are located in the subgroup of smaller mining power. Although possible this would limit the generality of the attack, because the attacker would be constrained on the transactions it can override.

Note that the Balance Attack inherently violates the persistence of the main branch prefix and is enough for the attacker to double spend. The attacker has simply to identify the subgroup that contains merchants and create transactions to buy goods from these merchants. After that, it can issue the transactions to this subgroup while propagating its mined blocks to at least one of the other subgroups. Once the merchant has shipped goods, the attacker stops delaying messages. Based on the high probability that the tree seen by the merchant is outweighed by another subtree, the attacker could reissue another transaction transferring the exact same coin again.

5.4 Double spending in Ethereum

In order to gain some insights regarding the public Ethereum blockchain we combined the name and block contributions of the top-10 mining pools as observed on `http://etherscan.io` during one week on August 3rd, 2017 with their network connectivity information in Fig. 5.2. To this end, to each named mining pool we registered a miner that could gather IP and *Autonomous System (AS)* information. ASes are groups of networks under the control of a single technical administration [HB96]. In particular, we estimated locations of the servers by querying five databases of IP geographic locations [DB, IP2, IP3, IP, IP4]. To reduce the inaccuracies of geographic locations, we extracted the location indicated in the majority of these databases. To retrieve the number and owner of each AS we relied on sources [CAI, Mer] based on the whois service. ASes have their own routing policy for internal traffic but use *Border Gateway Protocol (BGP)* [HRL06] for dynamic inter-AS routing. Unfortunately, BGP does not incorporate a mechanism to check whether an origin AS owns the IP prefixes that it announces. This makes the protocol vulnerable to route hijacking.

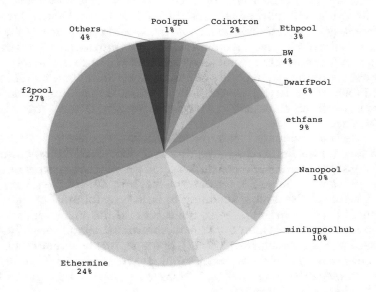

Fig. 5.2 The portions of mining power of the most powerful mining pools of Ethereum

5.4.1 Double spending is easy in case of route hijacking

To quantify the risk of a partitioning attack, we emulated the aforementioned Ethereum 10 most powerful mining pools by deploying 10 virtual machines (VMs) linked through five BGP routers controlled in our private cloud infrastructure via OpenStack. To obtain the mining power distribution of mining pools retrieved in Fig. 5.2 among our own VMs, we fixed the quantum of CPU time allocated to each machine using Linux control goups cgroups [Heo15]. The control groups allow us to specify the CPU quota Q that a VM can consume within a period of time T. Given the same value of T, we vary Q on all virtual machines based on their corresponding mining power percentage. As a result, we obtained the proportion we listed in Fig. 5.2 close to one decimal.

We then combined a BGP-hijacking attack with the balance attack [NG17] to evaluate the risks of double spending in Ethereum v1.5. First, the BGP hijacking is used to delay communication, then the balance attack is used to turn these delays into double spending. To this end, we assign the role of the adversary to one of the mining pool in each of our attack instances. The adversary takes control over one BGP router to prevent two ASes from communicating with two other ASes during 7 minutes. During that time, the adversary issues a transaction to one group and contributes to the block creation of the other group in order to discard its previously issued transaction. Since it is commonly recommended to wait for 12 confirmations to be confident about the immutability of a transaction since the version Homestead of Ethereum [But16b], we consider the double spending successful when the transactions contained in a block followed by 11 consecutive blocks gets discarded.

After the 7 minutes communication delay, we observed whether the adversary transaction is discarded due to the choice of the canonical chain in 30 consecutive runs and concludes upon the average success of the attack. As indicated in Table 5.1, we observe that only 10% of the mining power is sufficient for the double spending to be successful most of the time. With only 27% of the mining power, the success of the attack reaches 76%. This result confirms the claim from the literature that it is supposedly feasible to attack public blockchains [AZV17], however, this is without taking into account the nature of the network topology. We explain in Section 5.4.2 why the topology described in Fig. 5.2 makes the attack of the public Ethereum blockchain almost impossible.

5.4.2 Partitioning Ethereum mining pools turns out to be hard

While we showed that double spending could be easily achieved by partitioning public blockchains, it turns out that partitioning the mining power of Ethereum mining pools is actually very difficult.

Fig. 5.2 lists the stratum servers of the 10 most powerful Ethereum mining pools we retrieved. We noticed experimentally that if one of the stratum servers becomes unresponsive, then the corresponding miners would connect to the next stratum server they operate in order to remain connected to the pool. Hence, attempts to partition miners may lead miners to reconnect to a different AS.

In addition, it is more difficult to determine the precise proportion of mining power connected to each stratum server, again due to the numerous stratum servers each miner operates. Indeed, a mining pool identifier is nothing more than the wallet address to receive reward when a pool successfully mines a block. While it is possible to determine a block miner by examining header information, there is no way to pin down to the stratum server, as long as these servers put their reward into the same wallet address.

Table 5.1 Success of double spending with mining pools of similar power to the 10 most powerful Ethereum mining pools

Adversary mining power	Attacker subgroup mining power	Victim subgroup mining power	Double spending success
27%	34%	35%	77%
10%	43%	36%	57%

Second, the stratum servers typically hide the location of the mining pool participants, which makes it hard to isolate a group of pools of a specific mining power. Without information about the miners for a stratum server, one cannot guarantee the partition success of a network attack. It may *(i)* isolate a stratum server along with its miners completely, *(ii)* partition some miners, which reduces only a fraction of computational power from the pool, or *(iii)* cut off the connectivity between a stratum server and pool participants, such that those participants decide to reconnect to different stratum servers.

Third, BGP-hijacking cannot affect the direct interconnection between ASes, because ASes are aware of static network prefixes that belong to their peer ASes. Apart from exchanging routes at the *Internet Exchange Points (IXPs)*, any pair of ASes may decide to establish either layer 2 or layer 3 links to connect their networks directly. This prevents dynamic routing attacks like the BGP hijacking we discussed above in Section 5.4.1. To better understand the applicability of the attack to the Ethereum public blockchain, we retrieved the direct peering information of the eight ASes we identified using available information [CAI17] and their interconnections. Among the 10 most powerful public Ethereum mining pools, 7 of them solely rely on this group of ASes; together, they account for more than 87% of the total mining power of the network. As the majority of ASes in this group are linked by direct peering, it appears extremely difficult to partition Ethereum's overlay. For example, f2pool may send and update to ethfans via a peering connection, which in turn forwards the update to BW via another peering connection. Without an adversary gaining access to configuration on the border routers of these ASes, it will remain difficult to partition a pool from the rest of the group.

When given enough power, miners can be tempted to hack the blockchain to maximize their benefit. Some work have proposed to hold participants accountable for their actions, in order to mitigate this temptation. We discuss accountability in Section 5.6.

5.5 Proof-of-Authority and permissioned sealers of Ethereum

Proof-of-Authority (PoA) was recently proposed as a Byzantine fault toler-
ant consensus mechanism that integrates with the Ethereum protocol. The
Ethereum geth software offers two different consensus algorithms, called
Clique and Istanbul BFT whereas the Ethereum parity software offers the
consensus algorithm, called Aura. The concept is similar to traditional
Byzantine fault tolerant consensus in that only n sealers are permissioned
to create new blocks but requires authentication and strictly less than $\frac{n}{2}$
Byzantine participants. If Aura could be safe despite partial synchrony, then
it would be an ideal replacement to the Ethereum's default consensus algorithm we presented earlier.

5.5.1 The Aura algorithm

Algorithm 7 depicts the way Aura guarantees that participating nodes reach
consensus on the uniqueness of the block at a given index of the blockchain
in `parity`. Every participating node maintains a state comprising a set
of *sealers*, its current view of the blockchain c_i as a directed acyclic graph
$\langle B_i, P_i \rangle$, a block b with fields *parent* that links to the parent block, a *sealer* and
a *step* indicating the time at which the block is added to the blockchain, as
explained below. Initially, they are $\perp$ meaning "undefined".

The function propose() is invoked in order to propose a block for a particular index of the blockchain. The consensus is reached once the block
is decided, which can happen much later as we will explain in the function is-decided() (line 28) below. The algorithm discretises time into steps
that corresponds to consecutive periods of step-duration time, as specified in
a configuration file. Each sealer executes an infinite loop that periodically
checks whether the clock-time() indicates that this is its turn to propose a
block (line 13). When it is its turn (line 14), a sealer sets the parent of the
block to the last block of its view and signs it (line 16).

Each broadcast() invoked by the propose() function sends blocks that get
delivered to all other participating nodes that are honest (in reality only the
last block is broadcast unless some sealer is unaware of more blocks). The
deliver() function (line 24) is thus invoked at each honest participating node,
regardless of whether it is a sealer, upon reception of the broadcast message.
Once a blockchain view is delivered to p_i, the node compares the score of
the blockchain view it maintains to the blockchain view it receives, using
the score (line 21). The highest blockchain has the greatest score, however, if
two blockchains share the same height, then the one that is denser in terms
of its number of non-empty slots obtains the highest score. That is, among

---

Algorithm 7 The parity Aura algorithm at process p_i

1: **State:**
2:     *sealers* $\subseteq$ *Ids*, the set of sealers
3:     $c_i = \langle B_i, P_i \rangle$, the local blockchain at node p_i is a directed
4:        acyclic graph of blocks B_i and pointers P_i
5:     *b*, a block record with fields:
6:        *parent*, the block preceding b in the chain, initially $\perp$
7:        *sealer*, the sealer that signed block b, initially $\perp$
8:        *step*, the blockchain step when the block gets added, initially $\perp$
9:     step-duration, the duration of each step as configured
10:
11: propose()$_i$:
12:     **while** true **do**
13:        *step* $\leftarrow$ clock-time()/step-duration
14:        **if** $i \in$ *sealers* $\wedge$ *step* mod $|sealers| = i$) **then**
15:           $b.parent \leftarrow$ last-block(c_i)
16:           $b.sealer \leftarrow p_i$
17:           $c_i \leftarrow \langle B_i \cup \{b\}, P_i \cup \{b.parent\}\rangle$
18:           broadcast(c_i)
19:        sleep(step-duration)
20:
21: score($\langle B_j, P_j \rangle$):
22:     **return** UINT128_MAX $\times$ height($\langle B_j, P_j \rangle$) $-$ step-num($\langle B_j, P_j \rangle$)
23:
24: deliver($\langle B_j, P_j \rangle$)$_i$:
25:     **if** score($\langle B_j, P_j \rangle$) $>$ score($\langle B_i, P_i \rangle$) **then**
26:        $\langle B_i, P_i \rangle \leftarrow \langle B_j, P_j \rangle$
27:
28: is-decided(b)$_i$:
29:     $V \leftarrow \{b_k.sealer \mid b_k \in B_i; k \geq i\}$
30:     **return** ($|V| \times 2 > |sealers|$)

---

many blockchains with the same height, a blockchain whose last block has the the lowest index wins.

This is indicated by the two functions height and step-num that represent the height of the blockchain and the number of slots for which there exists a block in the blockchain.

5.5.2 The Attack of the Clones

Aura, just like Clique, is vulnerable to a particular attack, called the Attack of the Clone, that can lead to double spending. In particular, the clone is a malicious sealer that joins, with a duplicate identity, two groups of correct sealers in order to create two apparent majorities of sealers that progress to decide upon conflicting blocks.

By assumption, only a minority of the sealers can be malicious in Aura, this is the reason why Aura seems to need only a majority of sealed blocks to consider whether a block and its transactions appear to be committed. As we explain below, $(2 - (n \bmod 2))$ attacker(s) cloning their own instance into two clones are actually sufficient to double spend.

The first step of the attack of the clones is for some attacking sealer to duplicate its Ethereum instance into two clones. This consists for the malicious sealer of running two instances of the Ethereum protocol with the same address or public-private key pair. Note that these two instances could either share the same IP address or use distinct IP addresses. We call these two instances clones because one has the same information as the other during the whole duration of the attack. Ethereum allows these two cloned instances to both create blocks, however, as they use the same private key to seal blocks, they are considered to act as a unique sealer.

The attacker must exploit message delays between two groups of a minority of $\lceil n/2 \rceil - 1$ sealers, hence creating a transient partition. Recall that this can be achieved using the network attack presented in Section 5.4.1. At this moment, the two clones may not share exactly the same database content as they may not be aware of the exact same blocks that are present in the blockchain. To maintain the cloning at the start of the partition, the attacker copies the content of the blockchain database of one of the clones to the database of the other clone and connects each of these clones to a different partition.

In order to progress towards a double spending situation, each partition must commit transactions and thus decide blocks, this is why we need $(2 - (n \bmod 2))$ attackers that clone instances. There are now two cases to consider depending on whether the number n of sealers is odd or even. If n is odd, then the honest sealers can be split into two groups of $(n - 1)/2$ sealers, each representing a minority. Adding one clone to each minority is thus sufficient to obtain two majorities of $\lfloor n/2 \rfloor + 1$ sealers. If n is even, then with a single attacker $n - 1$ honest sealers would be split into two partitions of different sizes, one that contains $n/2$ sealers and another that contains $n/2 - 1$ sealers. Adding one clone in each partition would thus be insufficient to obtain two majorities, this is why we need $(2 - (n \bmod 2)) = 2$ attackers in this case.

In order to double spend, the attacker, say Alice, simply has to issue two conflicting transactions, one in each of the partition:

- T_A consists of Alice transferring all her coins to Bob whereas
- T_A' consists of Alice transferring all her coins to Carole.

The presence of the majority of sealers guarantees the progress of the protocol in both partitions so as to obtain the commit of a transaction T_A and T_A', even though they conflict. If these transaction buy goods, then the goods are ready to be shipped to Alice. When the communication is re-enabled, the adopted branch contains only one of the these transactions. The double spending has been successful.

5.6 Accountability

In traditional blockchain systems it is hard to track the behavior of participants. The problem of double spending relies precisely on the fact that some blocks vanish from the system during a fork resolution. This naturally prevents other participants from being able to hold attackers accountable for their double spending—as there is no longer traces of the double spending when it completes. This lack of accountability is one of the key reasons why blockchains are so often subject to attacks.

Accountability has been proposed in the context of peer-to-peer systems as a property of the distributed system that allows correct nodes to detect the malicious activities of other nodes, hence holding nodes responsible for their actions. Unfortunately, distributed system accountability is hard to achieve as it requires nodes, especially Byzantine ones, to participate in the protocol by sharing voluntarily their logs. When synchrony cannot be assumed then malicious nodes are incentivized to not share their log to remain undetected. In particular, no correct nodes is able to distinguish a slow network delaying a log message from a malicious node refusing to share its log.

The Accountable Byzantine Agreement has thus been proposed as the more specific problem of guaranteeing that consensus is reached when possible, when $f < n/3$, but to detect Byzantine nodes when a disagreement is reached. The key idea is for correct nodes to treat received messages to progress in the consensus towards a decision only if they receive a signed justification for these messages, i.e., that they satisfy the protocol. If no justification is provided, then the associated message is simply ignored. It is then sufficient to cross-check these justifications to identify who has misbehaved. If two conflicting messages were sent by the same sender, then this sender is identified as lying and the two conflicting messages constitute an undeniable proof-of-fraud. As a result, either malicious nodes do not justify themselves and no damages to the system happens, or they justify their messages and expose themselves to an eventual punishment.

The Accountable Byzantine Agreement problem is key to the security of blockchain systems, as accountability can incentivize nodes to behave correctly. Imagine a blockchain system that requests consensus participants to put assets on a deposit, under the control of the blockchain system, prior to participating. In a rationale model, it is reasonable to expect the consensus participants to accept to deposit assets given that they typically gain a reward when they help providing the service by for example creating new blocks. Consider that the blockchain system builds upon an accountable Byzantine agreement algorithm and compensates the losses resulting from double spending attacks by withdrawing assets from the Byzantine nodes that provoked this disagreement. In a rational model, a node will certainly think twice before taking the risk of losing its deposit before acting maliciously to try and double spend. This accountable Byzantine agreement thus makes the participants of the blockchain system accountable.

5.7 Conclusion

In this chapter, we presented full fledged attacks against blockchains that incorporate both a network attack and an asset loss using double spending. This attack has been evaluated against the Ethereum blockchain system in public, consortium and private contexts.

In the public context, on real-world data, we explain that, while such an attack is provably possible, the risks of succeeding in stealing assets remains extremely low on the existing Ethereum main chain. When Ethereum is deployed over a WAN in a consortium environment, however, we demonstrated that an adversary could more easily double-spend through BGP hijacking, with a double-spending success rate of up to 80%.

There exist a set of counter-measures to the attack presented above. The most effective one is perhaps to design solutions that do not require synchrony as messages cannot be all delivered in a known and fixed delay over large networks. We present such a solution in Chapter 6. Going one step further, counter-measures featuring accountability could disincentivize participants from misbehaving by generating proofs of fraud automatically, hence reducing the risks of success of such an attack.

5.8 Bibliographic notes

A survey of attacks against blockchain networks can be found in [NYGEV19] and network requirements have been listed before [DPS+14]. Many blockchains assume synchrony where all messages must be delivered in less than a known bounded time [Nak08, Woo15, LNZ+16, AMN+17, KKJG+17a, GHM+17, HMW18, ZMR18]. The drawback is that if some messages experience an unforeseen delay, then the blockchain guarantees are violated. Algorand [GHM+17] and Dfinity [HMW18] use randomization to restrict the task of deciding a block to a small subset. Elastico [LNZ+16] proposes a sharded consensus partitioned into sub-committees to run more but smaller scale consensus instances. RapidChain [ZMR18] improves Elastico's sharding by using a randomized selection and erasure coded gossip for scalability.

Other blockchains [KJG$^+$16, AMN$^+$17, KKJG$^+$17b, Roc18] assume synchrony for some operations, but use a Byzantine consensus that would work with partial synchrony [DLS88]. Solida [AMN$^+$17] assumes synchrony but builds upon PBFT [CL02]. Avalanche [Roc18] is analyzed under synchrony but is conjectured to work in a partially synchronous network. OmniLedger [KKJG$^+$17b] reorganizes nodes among shards using randomization to avoid attackers taking control of individual shards but needs an external consensus protocol. To assign participants to shard, Omniledger uses an identity protocol that requires synchronous communication channels.

Godel et al. [GKKT16] analyzed the effect of propagation delays on Bitcoin using a Markov process. Garay et al. [GKL15] investigated Bitcoin in the synchronous communication setting, however, this setting is often considered too restrictive [Cac01]. Pass et al. extended the analysis for when the bound on message delivery is unknown and showed in their model that the difficulty of Bitcoin's crypto-difficulty has to be adapted depending on the bound on the communication delays [PSS16].

The problem is that various attacks can be used to delay messages beyond the expected synchronous bound of all message delays: The fallacies of distributed computing were first proposed in the 90's by L. Peter Deutsch, and Bill Joy and Tom Lyon under the name of fallacies of networked computing. It has been extended later by James Gosling. Some statistics about the CERT/CC on the fact that network attacks have become commonplace can be found at https://www.cdrinfo.com/d7/content/certcc-statistics-1988-2004#incidents.

Several attacks benefited from an attacker able to attack the communication graph [PSS16, SZ15, NKMS16]. Decker and Wattenhoffer already observed that Bitcoin suffered from block propagation delays [DW13]. To hack blockchains without a significant mining power, hackers and researchers already thought of attacking the network [LS14, HKZG15, NG16b, NG17, EGJ20]. In 2014, a BGP hijacker exploited access to an ISP to steal US$83,000 worth of bitcoins by positioning itself between Bitcoin pools and their miners [LS14]. The Eclipse attack against Bitcoin [HKZG15] consists of isolating at the IP layer a victim miner from the rest of the network to exploit its resources by proposing new neighbors to a miner until it accepts to connect only to nodes under the control of the attacker. It showed that an attacker controlling 32 IP addresses could "eclipse" a Bitcoin node with 85% probability. While a Bitcoin node typically connects to 8 logical neighbors, an Ethereum node typically connects to 25 nodes, making the attack harder. The Blockchain Anomaly [NG16b] exploits message reordering in Ethereum to rollback committed transactions and double spend. The Balance Attack [NG17] partitions the network into groups of similar mining power to influence the selection of the canonical chain and double spend. Recently, actual man-in-the-middle attacks were run to demonstrate the feasibility of stealing assets in Ethereum without a significant mining power [EGJ18].

The Attack of the Clones and in particular its Aura algorithm pseudocode (Algorithm 7) is taken from [EGJ20]. This attack was acknowledged by the security team of Parity Technology and the security team of the Ethereum foundation and was also presented to the Ethereum development community [EGJ19]. The xDai blockchain of the POSDAO project has been working on the implementation of one of the counter-measures presented in [EGJ20].

The idea of accountability in distributed systems was pioneered by Haeberlen, Kuznetsov and Druschel [HKD07]. In a partially synchronous system, they guarantee that faulty processes will be suspected forever, though definitive evidence may not be obtained. The problem of Accountable Byzantine Agreement was defined in [CGG19, CGG21], and a solution called Polygraph for the partially synchronous system was proposed: it accurately detects at least $n/3$ Byzantine nodes when disagreement occurs. Polygraph is at the heart of the Long-Live Blockchain [RPG20] that recovers from forks by excluding Byzantine consensus nodes to tolerate more than $n/3$ Byzantine faults. Polygraph can be considered as the accountable variant of the Democratic BFT consensus algorithm [CGLR18] presented in Chapter 6.

Some techniques were also used to turn leader-based consensus algorithms into accountable consensus algorithms [SWN+21] but only if the number of faulty processes does not exceed $2n/3$, where n is the total number of processes. An efficient method [CGG+22a] transforms a consensus algorithm into an accountable consensus algorithm, however, it only works if the decision of all processes is expected to be identical. A more generic approach [CGG+22b] converts any non-synchronous protocol solving a decision task into a corresponding accountable protocol. Accountability has recently been used to solve consensus when less than $2n/3$ are correct [RG22] by exploiting game theory.

5.9 Exercises

Question 1

True or false? Synchronization is a realistic assumption when considering that communication occurs over the Internet.

Question 2

In communication synchrony, we assume two things. First, we assume that every message sent gets delivered in a maximum amount of time. What is the second assumption?

a. This maximum amount of time is not known by the algorithm
b. This maximum amount of time is known by the algorithm

Question 3

In classic blockchains, the chain can fork. What is the recommendation for users to consider that a transaction is committed?

a. To wait for 1 hour
b. To wait until they can see a number k of blocks are appended to the blockchain, the first of these blocks containing this transaction
c. To make sure this transaction is part of the first block observed at a particular index

Question 4

We learned of 8 well-known fallacies that people tend to have about distributed systems and networking. Regarding the network, which of the following did we learn is not true?

a. There is no single administrator
b. It is not reliable
c. It is homogenous
d. The network is not secure

Question 5

Regarding the speed and latency of the distributed systems and networking, which of the following is not correct?

a. Bandwidth is limited
b. There is no latency
c. Transport is costly
d. The network topology changes over time

Question 5

True or false? It is possible for a Byzantine node to double spend without owning a large portion of the mining power in proof of work blockchains.

Question 6

Let E3 be a set of edges that separates the communication graph in two subgraphs with same cumulative mining power. Let an attacker delay messages

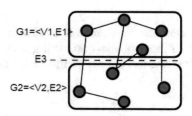

Fig. 5.3 A distributed execution with three processes

on E3. As the communication is delayed between the two subgraphs, each subgraph mines its own DAG. For an attacker who is connected to both subgraphs, he will need to mine a small number of blocks. To which subgraph(s) shall he contribute his blocks in order to double spend in this situation?

a. One subgraph
b. Both subgraphs

Question 7

Network attacks that enable to intercept messages in the network are often called what?

a. Sybil Attack
b. Man-in-the-middle attack
c. Rosenfeld?s attack
d. 51% attack

Question 8

True or false? Ethereum is vulnerable to man-in-the-middle attacks when run in a consortium environment.

Question 9

True or false? It is possible to double spend in a network running Ethereum when some messages are delayed for less than 5 minutes.

Question 10

True or false? It is impossible for the Balance Attack to succeed against Ethereum when the attacker has less than 1% of the mining power.

References

AMN⁺17.   Ittai Abraham, Dahlia Malkhi, Kartik Nayak, Ling Ren, and Alexander
           Spiegelman. Solida: A blockchain protocol based on reconfigurable byzan-
           tine consensus. In *Proc. of the 21st International Conference on Principles of Dis-
           tributed Systems, (OPODIS)*, pages 25:1–25:19, 2017.
AZV17.   Maria Apostolaki, Aviv Zohar, and Laurent Vanbever. Hijacking bitcoin:
           Routing attacks on cryptocurrencies. In *IEEE S&P 2017*, pages 375–392, 2017.
But16.   Vitalik Buterin. How should i handle blockchain forks in my dapp?, 1
           2016. https://ethereum.stackexchange.com/questions/183/how-should-i-
           handle-blockchain-forks-in-my-dapp/203/#203.
Cac01.   Christian Cachin. Distributing trust on the internet. In *Proceedings of the
           International Conference on Dependable Systems and Networks (DSN)*, pages 183–
           192, 2001.
CAI.   CAIDA: Center for Applied Internet Data Analysis.
CAI17.   The CAIDA AS Relationships Dataset, August 2017.
CGG19.   Pierre Civit, Seth Gilbert, and Vincent Gramoli. Polygraph: Accountable
           byzantine consensus. In *Workshop on Verification of Distributed Systems
           (VDS'19)*, Jun 2019.
CGG21.   Pierre Civit, Seth Gilbert, and Vincent Gramoli. Polygraph: Accountable
           byzantine agreement. In *Proceedings of the 41st IEEE International Conference
           on Distributed Computing Systems (ICDCS)*, pages 403–413, 2021.
CGG⁺22a.   Pierre Civit, Seth Gilbert, Vincent Gramoli, Rachid Guerraoui, and Jovan Ko-
           matovic. As easy as ABC: Optimal (A)ccountable (B)yzantine (C)onsensus
           is easy! In *Proceedings of the 36th IEEE International Parallel and Distributed
           Processing Symposium (IPDPS'22)*. IEEE, 2022.
CGG⁺22b.   Pierre Civit, Seth Gilbert, Vincent Gramoli, Rachid Guerraoui, Jovan Koma-
           tovic, Zarko Milosevic, and Adi Serendinschi. Crime and punishment in dis-
           tributed byzantine decision tasks. In *Proceedings of the 42nd IEEE International
           Conference on Distributed Computing Systems (ICDCS'22)*, 2022.
CGLR18.   Tyler Crain, Vincent Gramoli, Mikel Larrea, and Michel Raynal. DBFT: Effi-
           cient leaderless byzantine consensus and its applications to blockchains. In
           *Proceedings of the 17th IEEE International Symposium on Network Computing and
           Applications (NCA'18)*, 2018.
CL02.   Miguel Castro and Barbara Liskov. Practical byzantine fault tolerance and
           proactive recovery. *ACM Trans. Comput. Syst.*, 20(4):398–461, 2002.
DB.   DB-IP - IP Geolocation and Network Intelligence. https://db-ip.com/.
DLS88.   Cynthia Dwork, Nancy Lynch, and Larry Stockmeyer. Consensus in the pres-
           ence of partial synchrony. *J. ACM*, 35(2):288–323, April 1988.
DPS⁺14.   Maya Dotan, Yvonne-Anne Pignolet, Stefan Schmid, Saar Tochner, and Aviv
           Zohar. Survey on cryptocurrency networking: Context, state-of-the-art, chal-
           lenges. Technical Report 1409.6606, arXiv, 2014.
DW13.   Christian Decker and Roger Wattenhofer. Information propagation in the
           bitcoin network. In *Proc. of the IEEE International Conference on Peer-to-Peer
           Computing*, pages 1–10, 2013.
EGJ18.   Parinya Ekparinya, Vincent Gramoli, and Guillaume Jourjon. Impact of man-
           in-the-middle attacks on ethereum. In *SRDS*, 2018.
EGJ19.   Parinya Ekparinya, Vincent Gramoli, and Guillaume Jourjon. The attack of
           the clones against proof-of-authority. In *Community Ethereum Development
           Conference (EDCON'19)*, 2019.
EGJ20.   Parinya Ekparinya, Vincent Gramoli, and Guillaume Jourjon. The Attack
           of the Clones against Proof-of-Authority. In *Proceedings of the Network and
           Distributed Systems Security Symposium (NDSS'20)*. Internet Society, Feb 2020.

GHM+17.   Yossi Gilad, Rotem Hemo, Silvio Micali, Georgios Vlachos, and Nickolai Zel-
            dovich. Algorand: Scaling byzantine agreements for cryptocurrencies. In
            Proceedings of the 26th Symposium on Operating Systems Principles, SOSP '17,
            pages 51–68, 2017.

GKKT16.   J. Göbel, H.P. Keeler, A.E. Krzesinski, and P.G. Taylor. Bitcoin blockchain
            dynamics: The selfish-mine strategy in the presence of propagation delay.
            Performance Evaluation, Juy 2016.

GKL15.   Juan A. Garay, Aggelos Kiayias, and Nikos Leonardos. The bitcoin backbone
            protocol: Analysis and applications. In *Proceedings of the 34th Annual Inter-
            national Conference on the Theory and Applications of Cryptographic Technique
            (EUROCRYPT)*, pages 281–310, 2015.

HB96.   J. Hawkinson and T. Bates. Guidelines for creation, selection, and registration
            of an Autonomous System (AS), March 1996.

Heo15.   Tejun Heo. Control Group v2, October 2015. https://www.kernel.org
            /doc/Documentation/cgroup-v2.txt.

HKD07.   Andreas Haeberlen, Petr Kouznetsov, and Peter Druschel. PeerReview: Prac-
            tical accountability for distributed systems. *SOSP*, 2007.

HKZG15.   Ethan Heilman, Alison Kendler, Aviv Zohar, and Sharon Goldberg. Eclipse
            attacks on bitcoin's peer-to-peer network. In *24th USENIX Security Sympo-
            sium*, pages 129–144, 2015.

HMW18.   Timo Hanke, Mahnush Movahedi, and Dominic Williams. DFINITY technol-
            ogy overview series, consensus system. Technical Report 1805.04548, arXiv,
            May 2018.

HRL06.   Susan Hares, Yakov Rekhter, and Tony Li. A Border Gateway Protocol 4
            (BGP-4), January 2006.

IP.   IP Address to Identify Geolocation Information. http://www.ip2locat
            ion.com/.

IP2.   IP Address Details - ipinfo.io. http://ipinfo.io/.

IP3.   IP Address Geolocation to trace Country, Region, City, ZIP Code, etc. http
            s://www.eurekapi.com/.

IP4.   IP Geolocation and Online Fraud Prevention | MaxMind. https://www.
            maxmind.com/en/home.

KJG+16.   Eleftherios Kokoris Kogias, Philipp Jovanovic, Nicolas Gailly, Ismail Khoffi,
            Linus Gasser, and Bryan Ford. Enhancing bitcoin security and performance
            with strong consistency via collective signing. In *25th USENIX Security Sym-
            posium (USENIX Security 16)*, pages 279–296, Austin, TX, 2016. USENIX As-
            sociation.

KKJG+17a.   Eleftherios Kokoris-Kogias, Philipp Jovanovic, Linus Gasser, Nicolas Gailly,
            Ewa Syta, and Bryan Ford. Omniledger: A secure, scale-out, decentralized
            ledger. Technical Report 2017/405, Cryptology ePrint, 2017.

KKJG+17b.   Eleftherios Kokoris-Kogias, Philipp Jovanovic, Linus Gasser, Nicolas Gailly,
            Ewa Syta, and Bryan Ford. Omniledger: A secure, scale-out, decentralized
            ledger via sharding. Cryptology ePrint Archive, Report 2017/406, 2017. ht
            tps://eprint.iacr.org/2017/406.

LNZ+16.   Loi Luu, Viswesh Narayanan, Chaodong Zheng, Kunal Baweja, Seth Gilbert,
            and Prateek Saxena. A secure sharding protocol for open blockchains. In *Pro-
            ceedings of the 2016 ACM SIGSAC Conference on Computer and Communications
            Security*, CCS '16, pages 17–30, 2016.

LS14.   Pat Litke and Joe Stewart. BGP hijacking for cryptocurrency profit, August
            2014.

Mer.   Merit RADb. http://www.radb.net/.

Nak08.   Satoshi Nakamoto. Bitcoin: a peer-to-peer electronic cash system, 2008. ht
            tp://www.bitcoin.org.

NG16a.   Christopher Natoli and Vincent Gramoli. The balance attack against proof-
            of-work blockchains: The R3 testbed as an example. Technical Report
            1765133, arXiv, 2016.
NG16b.   Christopher Natoli and Vincent Gramoli. The blockchain anomaly. In *Pro-
            ceedings of the 15th IEEE International Symposium on Network Computing and
            Applications (NCA'16)*, pages 310–317, Oct 2016.
NG17.   Christopher Natoli and Vincent Gramoli. The balance attack or why forkable
            blockchains are ill-suited for consortium. In *Proceedings of the 47th IEEE/IFIP
            International Conference on Dependable Systems and Networks (DSN'17)*, June
            2017.
NKMS16.   Kartik Nayak, Srijan Kumar, Andrew Miller, and Elaine Shi. Stubborn min-
            ing: Generalizing selfish mining and combining with an eclipse attack. In
            *IEEE European Symposium on Security and Privacy, EuroS&P 2016, Saarbrücken,
            Germany, March 21-24, 2016*, pages 305–320, 2016.
NYGEV19.   Christopher Natoli, Jiangshan Yu, Vincent Gramoli, and Paulo Esteves-
            Verissimo. Deconstructing blockchains: A comprehensive survey on con-
            sensus, membership and structure. Technical Report 1908.08316, arXiv, 2019.
PSS16.   Rafael Pass, Lior Seeman, and Abhi Shelat. Analysis of the blockchain pro-
            tocol in asynchronous networks. Technical Report 454, Crytology ePrint
            Archive, 2016.
RG22.   Alejandro Ranchal-Pedrosa and Vincent Gramoli. TRAP: the bait of ratio-
            nal players to solve byzantine consensus. In Yuji Suga, Kouichi Sakurai,
            Xuhua Ding, and Kazue Sako, editors, *Proceedings of the ACM Asia Confer-
            ence on Computer and Communications Security (Asia CCS'22)*, pages 168–181.
            ACM, 2022.
Roc18.   Team Rocket. Snowflake to avalanche: A novel metastable consensus proto-
            col family for cryptocurrencies, 2018. Unpublished manuscript.
RPG20.   Alejandro Ranchal-Pedrosa and Vincent Gramoli. Blockchain is dead,
            long live blockchain! Accountable state machine replication for longlasting
            blockchain. Technical Report 2007.10541, arXiv, 2020.
SWN+21.   Peiyao Sheng, Gerui Wang, Kartik Nayak, Sreeram Kannan, and Pramod
            Viswanath. Bft protocol forensics. In *Computer and Communication Security
            (CCS)*, Nov 2021.
SZ15.   Yonatan Sompolinsky and Aviv Zohar. Secure high-rate transaction process-
            ing in bitcoin. In *Financial Cryptography and Data Security - 19th International
            Conference, FC 2015, San Juan, Puerto Rico, January 26-30, 2015, Revised Selected
            Papers*, pages 507–527, 2015.
Woo15.   Gavin Wood. Ethereum: A secure decentralised generalised transaction
            ledger, 2015. Yellow paper.
ZMR18.   Mahdi Zamani, Mahnush Movahedi, and Mariana Raykova. Rapidchain:
            Scaling blockchain via full sharding. Cryptology ePrint Archive, Report
            2018/460, 2018. https://eprint.iacr.org/2018/460.

Chapter 6
Making Blockchains Scale

> I understand democracy as
> something that gives the weak the
> same chance as the strong.
>
> *Mohandas Gandhi*

© Springer Nature Switzerland AG 2022
V. Gramoli, *Blockchain Scalability and its Foundations in Distributed Systems*,
https://doi.org/10.1007/978-3-031-12578-2_6

6.1 Introduction

In this chapter, we tackle the problem of *scalability* or the problem of preserving or improving a property as the system size increases. Scalability of
blockchain systems is a difficult problem as their properties often deterio-
rate with the system size. Their carbon footprint and the cumulative storage
space they consume typically enlarges as more miners enter the race of find-
ing the proof-of-work described in Chapter 3. However, their performance
does not necessarily improve.

In the face of this scalability issue affecting classic blockchain systems, a
series of overlying protocols were designed to minimize accesses to these
blockchains in what is referred to as layer 2, in comparison to the first layer
of the blockchains. The idea consists of redirecting the application to off-
chain computation when possible or organizing a hierarchy of blockchain
instances to not bloat the beacon or parent chain. Although appealing to
increase transaction throughput and minimize storage, it offers a way to
bypass the blockchain scalability problem rather than addressing it.

In this chapter, we present *Red Belly Blockchain*, a scalable blockchain system. Red Belly Blockchain does not suffer from the security vulnerabilities
presented in Chapter 5 because its guarantees are deterministic and it does
not require synchrony. Red Belly Blockchain differs from classic proof-of-
work blockchains presented in Chapter 3: it does not incentivize all nodes
to try to decide on every block, but rather allows every node to decide upon
some block. This means that only a subset of nodes are permissioned to run
the consensus algorithm regarding each block and as Red Belly Blockchain
throughput increases to up to hundreds of geodistributed consensus participants, this is enough for representing a fair distribution of nodes in all the
world jurisdictions.

To achieve this result, Red Belly Blockchain drastically revisits Byzantine Fault Tolerant (BFT) blockchains, getting rid of the predominant leader-
based design to decide multiple proposals and parallelizing the verification
of signatures. In particular, it builds upon the Democratic BFT consensus
algorithm, that aims at balancing the load of proposing new blocks on multiple nodes rather than concentrating it on a single leader node. To this
end, every node exploits a reliable broadcast primitive that propagates their
block to other nodes, before invoking a series of binary consensus whose
decisions indicate which reliably delivered blocks can be combined into a
superblock.

6.2 Consensus without synchrony

In Chapter 4, we have seen several algorithms that solve consensus while assuming synchrony, or that every message in the network takes less time to

be delivered than a known upper-bound. This synchrony assumption helps us solve the consensus problem since we know now that under asynchrony and failures, one would not be able to solve consensus. However, this assumption also makes the solution vulnerable to network attacks as we illustrated with the Balance Attack in Chapter 5. Partial synchrony (cf. Section 3.4.4) is another assumption not as strong as synchrony but that also offers the possibility to solve consensus. It allows to tolerate unpredictable network delays while always ensuring that no disagreement—and thus no forks—can occur as long as there are strictly less than $n/3$ failures. Recall that partial synchrony requires all messages to be delivered in a bounded but unknown amount of time.

6.2.1 The seminal Practical Byzantine Fault Tolerance

PBFT is a consensus protocol that works when assuming partial synchrony and when $n > 3f$. More precisely, PBFT is considered a state machine replication protocol because it can run a sequence of consecutive Byzantine consensus instances for nodes to agree upon the same sequence of commands to execute. Since its initial publication in 1999, it has been influential in the design and implementation of a large class of Byzantine consensus protocols (and their associated state machine replication protocol) for secure distributed systems outside the scope of blockchains. PBFT relies on a node that plays a special role, called the *leader*, in order to solve the classic Byzantine consensus problem of Definition 4.1. In particular, PBFT falls in the class of *leader-based consensus algorithms*, the consensus algorithms in which a unique leader node sends its proposal to all other nodes in order to collect votes on this particular proposal. A *leaderless consensus algorithm* is one that is not leader-based.

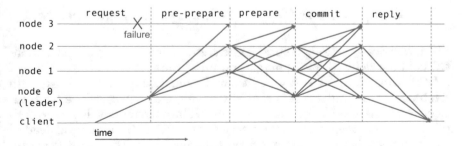

Fig. 6.1 The leader-based communication pattern of a good execution of PBFT involves a leader that relays the client request to the $n - 1$ followers so that a decision is taken by a correct node if $2f + 1$ distinct replicas committed the request.

A simple, yet ideal, execution of PBFT is represented in Figure 6.1 as a distributed execution where time increases from left to right, and where a client sends a request to a leader that requires the participation of $2f + 1$ servers, including itself, to decide upon this request. In this execution, one server, called node 3, is Byzantine and fails by crashing while the other nodes are correct. Note that the executions of the PBFT algorithm can be more elaborate: for example, the algorithm includes a view-change mechanism to change from one leader to another in case the leader is suspected to be faulty. Unfortunately, there is no way to detect whether a node is faulty, and a wrong suspicion can thus lead to a performance overhead induced by such a view-change.

6.2.2 Complexities

If the leader of PBFT is suspected by the other participants to be faulty, then a view-change procedure (not presented in Figure 6.1) starts to replace the leader in a round-robin fashion. To make sure that a new view will not prepare a different value from the one committed in a previous view, some information should be propagated across consecutive views. As the view-change rotates among at most $f + 1$ nodes to elect a correct leader, there are at most $f + 1$ view-change rounds before termination, hence leading to a time complexity of $O(f)$.

The message in each round is broadcast by n nodes leading to a message complexity of $O(fn^2)$.

The message in each view-change round contains the state received from the previous view-change rounds, which is at most $O(f)$ bits. As there are up to $O(fn^2)$ of these messages, the bit complexity is $O(f^2n^2)$ bits.

6.2.3 Changes required by the scale of the consensus network

PBFT was designed long before blockchain was invented, and was demonstrated on a network file system application running on four machines of a Local Area Network (LAN). This small scale deployment contrasts with the blockchain context that is typically a wide area network. The large variety of off-the-shelf PBFT-like protocols led blockchain developers to simply build their blockchain upon variants of PBFT, all inheriting its leader-based pattern that was shown instrumental for LANs. The question we answer below is whether this centralized design decision prevents these secure blockchains from scaling to wider networks.

6.3 Leveraging bandwidth

The inherent centralization of leader-based consensus algorithms makes these algorithms heavily dependent on the resources of the unique particular node that plays the role of the leader. The leader can act as a bottleneck when the distributed system enlarges or as the number of consensus participants increases. The view-change procedure that replaces a suspicious leader is typically difficult to implement and thus error-prone. The leader also makes the protocols vulnerable to denial-of-service attacks, where flooding the current leader is sufficient to stop the service. This is why coping with the problem induced by a leader has been an active area of research for decades. We illustrate below a reason why the leader can act as a bottleneck by comparing the time complexity of propagating a proposal in a leader-based design (as in the pre-prepare phase of PBFT depicted in Fig. 6.1) and a leaderless design that will be presented in detail in Section 6.5.

6.3.1 The time complexity of a leader-based propagation

Let us introduce a simple example to demonstrate the problem of the leader bottleneck and illustrate the advantage of a more distributed alternative. Consider a blockchain service that relies on PBFT for participating nodes to decide upon the next block to be appended to the blockchain. In a leader-based consensus protocol, the leader proposes a block to all the other nodes, as indicated by the one-to-all message exchange of Figure 6.1, and tries to gather sufficiently many votes in order to decide this block. We can already anticipate that the sending of this block to all nodes will have a cost imposed by the resources of the leader: for the consensus to be reached fast, the leader should send this value to all other nodes as fast as possible. Although this broadcast can be implemented efficiently in a LAN through the data link layer, it cannot be done in a Wide Area Network (WAN) where there is no broadcast support. Instead, the leader will have to send a separate copy of this block to each individual node, a task whose execution time increases with the number of nodes.

More formally, consider a block of B bits and a blockchain system with n nodes with limited bandwidth resources. In particular, each node i is equipped with a download capacity of d_i and an upload capacity of u_i, both expressed in bits per unit of time. Without loss of generality, let the leader be process 1 with capacities d_1 and u_1. The time P it will take the leader to send the block to all nodes (we consider that the leader sends to itself for simplicity) is the maximum between these two:

- The time for the leader to upload nB bits, which is $\frac{nB}{u_1}$.

- The time to download B bits for the node that has the lowest download rate among all other nodes, which is $\frac{B}{min(d_i:1\leq i\leq n)}$.

Hence the time it takes for the leader to propagate the block to all nodes is $P = max\left(\frac{nB}{u_1}, \frac{B}{min(d_i:1\leq i\leq n)}\right)$ and we can conclude that this time is $\Omega(n)$.

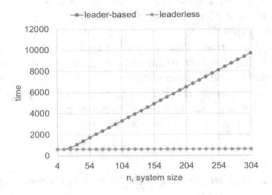

Fig. 6.2 The time it takes for propagating a block in a leader-based consensus algorithm typically increases with the number of nodes whereas the time to propagate a block in a leaderless consensus algorithm is independent of n.

6.3.2 The time complexity of a leaderless propagation

To contrast the leader-based approach with a more 'decentralized' baseline, consider an hypothetical leaderless consensus protocol where all nodes propose values that can be decided. The example of such an algorithm is deferred to Section 6.5. Hence, let every node send B/n bits to each other for each of them to receive the same block of B bits as in the previous example. The time P' it takes for a leaderless protocol to exchange this block is the maximum of these two values:

- The time for the node with the lowest upload rate to upload B/n bits, which is $\frac{B/n}{min(u_i:1\leq i\leq n)}$.
- The time for the node with the lowest download rate to download B bits, which is $\frac{B}{min(d_i:1\leq i\leq n)}$.

Hence, the time it takes for the leaderless protocol to propagate the block to all nodes is $P' = max\left(\frac{B/n}{min(u_i:1\leq i\leq n)}, \frac{B}{min(d_i:1\leq i\leq n)}\right)$, which does not increase linearly with n. In other words, the performance of a leader-based algorithm degrades with the size of the network, but it is not necessarily the case for leaderless algorithms as explained below.

6.3.3 Bypassing the leader bottleneck with the superblock optimization

To illustrate the degradation of performance of the leader-based algorithm, Figure 6.2 depicts the time it would take to propagate a block of B bits in a system where the leader has a 10 times higher upload rate than any other node and where every node downloads twice faster than it can upload. When the system is small, the time it takes for a leader-based propagation of B bits is similar to the time it takes for a leaderless propagation of B bits, however, when the system size exceeds 21, then the leaderless protocol starts being faster and the difference in performance increases as the system grows. This illustrates an inherent lack of scalability in traditional leader-based designs induced by a bottleneck effect: the limited resources of the leader.

To conclude, a fundamental limitation of the leader-based consensus algorithm stems from the need for one node to propose its value of B bits to the rest of the nodes: at the end of the consensus algorithm execution, only this value can be decided. Of course, some tentatives may fail and other leaders might be elected one after another, but in the end the value decided is the value proposed by the chosen leader. By contrast, the leaderless consensus algorithm benefits from having multiple nodes proposing B/n bits and the possibility for the decided value to combine all these n proposed values into one large decided value of size B. In the context of blockchain, the values can be called blocks, hence we say that combining n proposed blocks, each of size B/n, results into a *superblock* of size B. This optimization of bypassing the leader bottleneck is thus called the *superblock optimization*.

6.4 The Set Byzantine Consensus problem

It is interesting to note that the classic definition of the consensus problem does not allow the superblock optimization. In particular, solving consensus generally requires to satisfy a validity property that states that the value decided must be one of the values that were proposed. As an example, recall the validity property of the previous consensus definition (Def. 4.1): this validity is not satisfied by the superblock optimization as the decided value can be none of the proposed value; the decided value results from the combination of multiple proposed values. This is the reason why we need a new definition for the consensus problem, called the Set Byzantine Consensus

(Def. 6.1) problem, that relaxes the classic validity requirement to allow for the superblock optimization.

Definition 6.1 (Set Byzantine Consensus). Assuming that each correct node proposes a proposal, the *Set Byzantine Consensus* (SBC) problem is for each of them to decide on a set in such a way that the following properties are satisfied:

- SBC-Termination: every correct node eventually decides a set of transactions;
- SBC-Agreement: no two correct nodes decide on different sets of transactions;
- SBC-Validity: a decided set of transactions is a non-conflicting set of valid transactions taken from the union of the proposed sets; and if all nodes are correct and propose the same set of non-conflicting valid transactions, then this subset is the decided set.

The SBC-Termination and SBC-Agreement properties are common to many Byzantine consensus definition variants, while SBC-Validity is different: it includes two predicates, the first states that transactions proposed by Byzantine proposers could be decided as long as they are correctly signed and non conflicting; the second one is necessary to prevent any trivial algorithm that decides a pre-determined value from solving the problem.

So why is the Set Byzantine Consensus not the classic definition of the consensus problem? There are several reasons. First, consensus is an old problem defined in the 80's at which time the key challenge was not to make a software run on a distributed system of thousands of machines. Second, the classic definition gave a uniform description of three properties whose simplicity had a pedagogical advantage. Third, blockchain did not exist at that time and researchers were trying to find a practical Byzantine fault tolerant consensus implementation that could run within a network file system on four nodes. Once discovered this protocol influenced a long series of Byzantine fault tolerant systems that all inherit the same leader-based design as listed in Section 6.8. Below, we explain how to solve the Set Byzantine Consensus with a leader-less consensus algorithm for large-scale blockchain systems.

6.5 Democratic Byzantine fault tolerance

The Democratic Byzantine fault tolerance (DBFT) consists of avoiding the bottleneck effect of the leader by simply avoiding any particular process trying to impose its proposal. DBFT relies on a reduction from the binary Byzantine consensus to the multivalue consensus and is also time optimal, resilience optimal and does not use classic (strong) coordinator, which means that it does not wait for a particular message. In addition, it finishes in only 4 message delays in the good case, when all correct processes propose the same value. Note that the original DBFT algorithm [CGLR18] solves the classic Byzantine consensus we mentioned in Chapter 4. As we will see in Section 6.6, in order for DBFT to solve the Set Byzantine Consensus (Definition 6.1) we propose to merge the acceptable proposals into the final decision.

6.5.1 The binary Byzantine consensus problem

We first give the definition of the Binary Byzantine Consensus (BBC) problem.

Definition 6.2 (Binary Byzantine Consensus). Assuming that each correct process proposes a binary value in $\{0, 1\}$, the Binary Byzantine consensus problem is for each of them to decide on a value in such a way that the following properties are satisfied:

1. Termination: every correct node eventually decides.
2. Agreement: no two correct nodes decide differently.
3. BBC-Validity. If all correct processes propose the same value, no other value can be decided.

6.5.2 The binary Byzantine consensus algorithm of DBFT

For the sake of simplicity in the presentation, we present a safe version of the binary Byzantine consensus in Algorithm 8, a safe and live version is deferred to Section 6.6.

As depicted in Algorithm 8, process p_i proposes its initial binary value v_i by invoking bin_propose(v_i) at line 1. It then sets its estimate to its value (line 2) and initializes the round number r (line 3) before it can decide a value v by invoking decide(v) at line 14 within an asynchronous round (lines 4–15). Each of these asynchronous rounds comprises three phases depicted below:

Phase 1: Discard estimates proposed exclusively by Byzantine processes. Process p_i increments the round number at line 5. It then invokes an existing reliable broadcast protocol applied to binary values, called bv-broadcast (lines 16–22), that discards all the values proposed exclusively by Byzantine processes [MMR15b]. Note that this call is non-blocking, hence it executes in the background once the next line is reached. Symbol $\rightarrow$ indicates that

Algorithm 8 The safe binary Byzantine consensus algorithm of DBFT

1: bin-propose(val):
2:     $est \leftarrow val$
3:     $r \leftarrow 0$
4:     **repeat:**
5:         $r \leftarrow r + 1$
6:         bv-broadcast(EST$[r], val, i$) $\rightarrow$ *bin-values*$[r]$
7:         **wait until** (*bin-values*$[r] \neq \varnothing$)
8:         broadcast(AUX$[r]$, *bin-values*$[r], i$) $\rightarrow$ *favorites*$[r]$
9:         **wait until** $\exists$*values* $\subseteq$ *favorites*$[r]$ where the following conditions hold:
10:             • **if** v received in AUX msgs of $n - t$ processes **then** $v \in$ *values*
11:             • $\forall v \in$ *values*, $v \in$ *bin-values*$[r]$
12:         **if** (*values* $= \{v\}$) **then**
13:             $est \leftarrow v$
14:             **if** $v = (r \bmod 2)$ and no previous decision by p_i **then** decide(v)
15:         **else** $est \leftarrow (r \bmod 2)$

16: bv-broadcast(MSG, val, i):
17:     broadcast(BV, $\langle val, i \rangle$)
18:     **repeat:**
19:         **if** (BV, $\langle v, * \rangle$) received from ($f + 1$) processes but not yet re-broadcast **then**
20:             broadcast(BV, $\langle v, i \rangle$)
21:         **if** (BV, $\langle v, * \rangle$) received from ($2f + 1$) processes **then**
22:             *bin-values* $\leftarrow$ *bin-values* $\cup \{v\}$

the array *bin-values*$_i$ gets populated in the background by all concurrent bv-broadcasts (line 6) at index r for round r.

During the bv-broadcast (lines 16–22), every correct process counts the number of distinct processes from which it receives each binary value and re-broadcasts the value(s) received from at least $f + 1$ distinct processes knowing that they are necessarily coming from at least one correct process (line 19). Finally, each of them "delivers" each value received by $2f + 1$ distinct processes by adding it to the set *bin-values*$_i$ so that for all correct processes p_j, *bin-values*$_j$ eventually contains all values broadcast by correct processes but no values broadcast only by Byzantine processes. Note that we do re-broadcast at line 20 the value received even if it was broadcast by the same process at line 17.

Phase 2: Identify values as sufficiently represented proposals. This second phase runs between lines 8 and 11. In this phase, p_i broadcasts normally (i.e., without using a reliable or binary value broadcast primitive) a message AUX$[r]$ whose content is *bin-values*$_i[r]$ (line 8) and delivers the broadcast messages it received from other processes by adding them to *favorites*$_i$.

Then, p_i waits until it has received a set of values *values*$_i$ satisfying the two following properties:

1. The values in $values_i$ come from the messages $\text{AUX}[r]$ of at least $(n - f)$ different processes.
2. The values in $values_i$ are included in the set $bin\text{-}values_i[r]$. Thanks to the bv-broadcast that filters out Byzantine value, even if Byzantine processes send fake $\text{AUX}[r]$ messages containing values proposed only by Byzantine processes, $values_i$ will contain only values broadcast by some correct process.

Hence, at any round r, after line 11, $values_i$ is included in $\{0, 1\}$ and contains only the initial binary values of correct processes.

Phase 3: Deciding the estimate upon convergence. The third phase runs between lines 12 and 15. This phase is a local computation phase, during which (if not done yet) p_i tries at line 14 to decide a value v that depends on the content of $values_i$ and the parity of the round.

1. If $values_i$ contains a single element v (line 12), then v becomes p_i's new estimate at line 13 and a candidate for the consensus decision. To ensure BBC-Agreement, v can be decided only if $v = r \bmod 2$. The decision is taken by the statement decide(v) at line 14.
2. If $values_i = \{0, 1\}$, then p_i cannot decide. As both values have been proposed by correct processes, p_i selects the parity of the round $r \bmod 2$, which is the same at all correct processes, as its new estimate (line 15).

Let us observe that the invocation of decide(v) by p_i does not terminate the participation of p_i in the algorithm, namely p_i continues looping forever. This is because a deciding process may need to help other processes converging to the decision in the two subsequent rounds. For the terminating version of this algorithm, refer to Algorithm 12.

6.5.3 Safety proof of the binary Byzantine consensus

The proof is described from a point of view of a correct process p_i. Let $values_i^r$ denote the value of the set $values_i$ which satisfies both the predicate of lines 12 and 13 when invoked at line 11 during a round r. We now restate the properties of BV-broadcast [MMR15b] using the notations presented at lines 16–22 of Algorithm 8.

Definition 6.3 (BV-broadcast). The bv-broadcast ensures the following properties:

- BV-Obligation: If at least $(f + 1)$ correct processes bv-broadcast the same value v, then v is eventually delivered to the set $bin\text{-}values_i$ of each correct process p_i;
- BV-Justification: If a correct process p_i delivers v, then v has been bv-broadcast by a correct process;

- BV-Uniformity: If a correct process p_i delivers v, then v is eventually delivered at all correct processes;
- BV–Termination: Eventually all correct processes deliver some value.

Lemma 6.1. *If at the beginning of a round r, all correct processes have the same estimate v, they never change their estimate value thereafter.*

Proof. Let us assume that all correct processes (which are at least $n - f > f + 1$) have the same estimate v when they start round r. Hence, they all BV-broadcast the same message $\text{EST}[r](v)$ at line 6. It follows from the BV-Justification and BV-Obligation properties that each correct process p_i is such that $bin\text{-}values_i[r] = \{v\}$ at line 7, and consequently can broadcast only $\text{AUX}[r](\{v\})$ at line 8. Considering any correct process p_i, it then follows from the predicate of line 11 ($values_i$ contains only v), the predicate of line 12 ($values_i$ is a singleton), and the assignment of line 14, that est_i keeps the value v.

The next lemma states that if the set $values$ in the same round of two correct processes are singletons then they are identical.

Lemma 6.2. *Let p_i and p_j be two correct processes. $((values[r]_i = \{v\}) \wedge (values[r]_j = \{w\})) \Rightarrow (v = w)$.*

Proof. Let p_i be a correct process such that $values[r]_i = \{v\}$. It follows from line 11 that p_i received the same message $\text{AUX}[r](\{v\})$ from $(n - f)$ different processes, i.e., from at least $(n - 2f)$ different correct processes. As $n - 2f \geq f + 1$, this means that p_i received the message $\text{AUX}[r](\{v\})$ from a set Q_i including at least $(f + 1)$ different correct processes.

Let p_j be a correct process such that $values[r]_j = \{w\}$. Hence, p_j received $\text{AUX}[r](\{w\})$ from a set Q_j of at least $(n - f)$ different processes. As $(n - f) + (f + 1) > n$, it follows that $Q_i \cap Q_j \neq \emptyset$. Let $p_k \in Q_i \cap Q_j$. As $p_k \in Q_i$, it is a correct process. Hence, at line 8, p_k sent the same message $\text{AUX}[r](\{\})$ to p_i and p_j, and we consequently have $v = w$.

Theorem 6.1 (BBC-Validity). *Let $f < n/3$. The value decided by a correct process was proposed by a correct process.*

Proof. Let us consider the round $r = 1$. Due to the BV-Justification property of the BV-broadcast of line 6, it follows that the sets $bin\text{-}values_i[1]$ contains only values proposed by correct processes. Consequently, the correct processes broadcast at line 8 messages $\text{AUX}[1]()$ containing sets with values proposed only by correct processes. It then follows from the predicate of line 11 ($values[1]_i \subseteq bin\text{-}values_i[1]$), and the BV-Justification property of the BV-broadcast abstraction, that the set $values[1]_i$ of each correct process contains only values proposed by correct processes. Hence, the assignment of est_i (be it at line 13 or 15) provides it with a value proposed by a correct process. The same reasoning applies to rounds $r = 2$, $r = 3$, etc., which concludes the proof of the lemma.

Theorem 6.2 (Agreement). *Let $f < n/3$. No two correct processes decide different values.*

Proof. Let r be the first round during which a correct process decides, let p_i be a correct process that decides in round r (line 14), and let v be the value it decides. Hence, we have $values[r]_i = \{v\}$ where $v = (r \bmod 2)$.

If another correct process p_j decides during round r, we have $values[r]_j = \{w\}$, and, due to Lemma 6.4, we have $w = v$. Hence, all correct processes that decide in round r, decide v. Moreover, each correct process that decides in round r has previously assigned $v = (r \bmod 2)$ to its local estimate est_j.

Let p_j be a correct that does not decide in round r. As $values[r]_i = \{v\}$, and p_j does not decide in round r, it follows from Lemma 6.4 that we cannot have $values[r]_j = \{1 - v\}$, and consequently $values[r]_j = \{0, 1\}$. Hence, in round r, p_j executes line 13, where it assigns the value $(r \bmod 2) = v$ to its local estimate est_j.

It follows that all correct processes start round $(r + 1)$ with the same local estimate $v = r \bmod 2$. Due to Lemma 6.3, they keep this estimate value forever. Hence, no different value can be decided in a future round by a correct process that has not decided during round r, which concludes the proof of the lemma.

6.6 Red Belly Blockchain

Recently, a new blockchain appeared particularly promising, the Red Belly Blockchain.[1] It relies on DBFT (Section 6.5) that solves the Set Byzantine Consensus problem (Definition 6.4) and scales to large networks by exploiting resources appropriately.

This section presents the two main design features of RBBC: its verification leverages the few computational resources when the system is small and its consensus leverages communication to commit more transactions when the system is large and bandwidth becomes limited. Although we call them 'sharding' techniques, all deciders decide the same set of transactions as opposed to traditional sharded blockchains [LNZ$^+$16, ZMR18].

6.6.1 Reducing the computation at small scale

Verification is needed to guarantee that the *Unspent Transaction Output (UTXO)* transactions [Nak08] are correctly signed. As verifications are CPU-intensive and notably affect performance, we shard the verification by letting different verifiers verify distinct transactions without reducing security.

---
[1] http://poseidon.it.usyd.edu.au/~concurrentsystems/rbbc/.

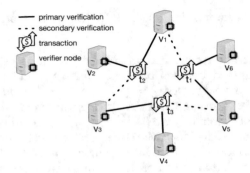

Fig. 6.3 The sharded verification with $n = 6$ and $f = 1$ where each transaction is verified by $f + 1$ (2 in this example) primary verifier nodes linked to this transaction with a solid line, before being verified only if necessary by f (1 in this example) secondary verifier nodes linked to this transaction with a dashed line

The expected result is twofold. First, it improves performance as it reduces each verifier computational load. Second, it helps scaling by further reducing the per-verifier computational load as the number of verifiers increases. We confirmed empirically [CNG18] that this can reduce the verification load to a third of what it would be without verification sharding.

As f verifier nodes can be Byzantine, each transaction signature has to be checked by at least $f + 1$ verifier nodes. If all the $f + 1$ nodes are unanimous in that the signature check passes, then at least one correct node checked the signature successfully and it follows that the transaction is guaranteed to be correct. Given that f nodes may be Byzantine, a transaction may need to be verified by up to $2f + 1$ times before $f + 1$ equal responses are computed. This is why we map each transaction to $f + 1$ *primary verifiers* and f *secondary verifiers*, hence summing up to $2f + 1$ verifiers.

The sharded verification consists of assigning proposals to two groups of nodes, $f + 1$ primary verifiers and f secondary verifiers as depicted in Figure 6.3. At the beginning of the consensus, every proposer node broadcasts its set of transactions to all permissioned nodes. Once a node receives one of the proposals for which it is a primary verifier, it immediately verifies the transactions of these proposals and broadcasts the outcome of the verification to all. As soon as a secondary verifier of a transaction detects that its $f + 1$ primary verifiers did not sent the same outcome, it verifies this proposal itself and broadcasts the outcome.

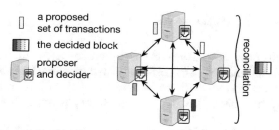

Fig. 6.4 Blockchain consensus executed by $n = 4$ proposers among which $t = 1$ is Byzantine: they propose sets of transactions (depicted with gray rectangles) and the decided value (on the right-hand side) is actually a block containing the union of all verified and non-conflicting transactions from the sets that were proposed (including potentially the set proposed by the Byzantine node)

6.6.2 Leveraging bandwidth at larger scales

In a large scale environment, geodistributed proposers are likely to receive different sets of transactions coming from requesters located in their vicinity. Instead of selecting one of these sets as the next block and discarding the others, RBBC combines all the sets of transactions proposed by distinct servers into a unique superblock to improve the performance (as we quantify empirically in [CNG18]).

In particular, RBBC decides upon multiple proposed sets of transactions. To illustrate why this is key for scalability, consider that each of the n proposers proposes $O(1)$ transactions. As opposed to blockchains based on traditional Byzantine consensus that will decide $O(1)$ transactions, RBBC can decide $\Omega(n)$ transactions. As the typical communication complexity of Byzantine consensus is $O(n^4)$ bits [CL02, CGLR18], it results that $O(n^3)$ bits are needed per committed transaction in RBBC, instead of $O(n^4)$.

To illustrate how RBBC achieves this optimization, consider Figure 6.4 that depicts $n = 4$ permissioned nodes that propose different sets of transactions but that decide a value that is actually a superblock containing the union of all sets of transactions that were proposed. It results from this optimization that the number of transactions decided grows linearly in n as long as each proposer proposes disjoint sets of valid transactions.

When the consensus is about to output the sets of transactions to be decided, some of these transactions may not be executable. For example, if these transactions withdraw a cumulative amount from an address that exceeds its remaining balance. Thus before deciding on the superblock, a deterministic reconciliation is performed at every node in lexicographical order of the transactions in the decided sets as detailed in Section 6.6.4.3.

6.6.3 *Assigning roles to nodes*

Here we explain how node roles are assigned for each transaction using a deterministic function. For each consensus instance, we have an ordered set P of permissioned node identifiers where $f + 1 \leq |P| < n$, indicating the nodes that play the role of primary or secondary proposers for all transactions.

For a requester to identify the proposer nodes responsible to propose a given transaction tx to the consensus, each node can execute a deterministic function $\mu(a)$ that takes as input the source account a of transaction tx and returns the identifier of a node $p_i \in P$, called the *primary proposer* of transaction tx. To guarantee that a transaction is proposed despite a faulty primary proposer, between f and $n - 1$ secondary proposers distinct from p_i are also selected deterministically. The number of proposers of each transaction tx is at least $f + 1$ to guarantee that tx will be proposed by at least one correct node. The number of proposers can be as large as n, however, fewer proposers lower latency whereas more proposers increase throughput, as we experimented in [CNG18].

As each transaction must be verified between $f + 1$ and $2f + 1$ times, each proposer p_i is also mapped to a set of $f + 1$ *primary_verifiers*$_{p_i}$ and a set of f additional *secondary_verifiers*$_{p_i}$. The *primary_verifiers*$_{p_i}$ include p_i itself and verify upon reception the signatures of tx. If the verification returns the same $f + 1$ results, then it becomes clear whether the signature of tx is correct. If not, f additional verifications are needed to identify the majority of $f + 1$ identical responses indicating whether the signature of tx is correct. This is why, the *secondary_verifiers*$_{p_i}$ set includes nodes of P that are distinct from the *primary_verifiers*$_{p_i}$ and that verify tx in case one or more of the primary verifiers are faulty or slow. More verifiers can be selected but would waste CPU resources.

In the absence of proof-of-work, Red Belly Blockchain needs a different mechanism to select which nodes have the permission to run the consensus at a particular index of the chain. This can be done in various ways: randomly by selecting a subset of public keys as it is done with sortition [GHM+17], by having the permissioned nodes at the previous index voting anonymously [CCCG20] or by selecting a subset of the nodes that have the largest stake as it is done with proof-of-stake, etc. Although not described here, the act of changing the set of nodes is done through consensus as explained in the community blockchains [VG19a].

6.6.4 From DBFT to Red Belly Blockchain

We now present how to build upon DBFT (Section 6.5) to build the Red Belly Blockchain. Algorithm 9 depicts the variant of DBFT that combines the blocks proposed by multiple validators into a superblock. For each proposal delivered at proposer p_i by the verified reliable broadcasts (Section 6.6.4.2), p_i participates in a binary consensus instance with value 1 (line 6). Proposer p_i proposes 0 to the remaining binary consensus instances (line 8) after a timer expires. This timer (line 3) increases with the age of the oldest transaction of the mempool to potentially decide it.

Algorithm 9 The DBFT Byzantine consensus algorithm with the superblock optimization

---

1: propose(val):
2:     (verified-)reliable-broadcast(val) $\rightarrow$ *props*
3:     start-timer(age of oldest tx in mempool)
4:     **while** $\nexists k : bitmask[k] = 1$ or *timer* did not expire **do**
5:        **for all** k such that $props[k]$ has been delivered
6:           $bitmask[k] \leftarrow$ bin-propose$_k(1)$
7:     **for all** k such that $props[k]$ has not been delivered
8:        $bitmask[k] \leftarrow$ bin-propose$_k(0)$
9:     **wait until** $bitmask$ is full and $\forall \ell, bitmask[\ell] = 1 : props[\ell] \neq \varnothing$
10:    reconciliate($bitmask$ & $props$)

All binary consensus instances proceed in parallel (their invocation is non-blocking). The decisions of these binary consensus instances constitute a *bitmask* that is applied to the set of potentially decidable proposals (line 10). Although the array of verified proposals may differ across correct nodes, the bitmasks of all correct nodes are guaranteed to contain 1s and be identical due to the agreement properties of the binary consensus. Note that even though the proposal may not be known yet for some of these indices, it is guaranteed by the reliable broadcast to be eventually delivered at all correct proposers (Section 6.6.4.2). Each correct proposer waits until a decidable proposal has been delivered at each of these indices (line 9), then each correct proposer obtains the same set of proposals after applying the *bitmask*.

6.6.4.1 Modifications

We modify Ben-Or, Kelmer and Rabin's reduction (lines 1–10) of the multivalue consensus problem to the binary consensus problem [BOKR94] to solve the Set Byzantine Consensus (Section 6.4) by replacing the reliable broadcast by our verified reliable broadcast (Section 6.6.4.2) and invoking a reconciliation to decide a superblock of non-conflicting transactions.

6.6.4.2 Verified all-to-all reliable broadcast

The verified reliable broadcast is a new reliable broadcast that delivers only successfully verified transactions. Algorithm 10 depicts the pseudocode of the verifiable reliable broadcast algorithm. In order for proposers to exchange verified proposals we add a `secp256k1` *Elliptic Curve Digital Signature Algorithm (ECDSA)* verification step to the reliable broadcast. Originally, the reliable broadcast is a 3-step one-to-all communication abstraction where any message delivered to a correct node gets eventually delivered to all correct nodes [Bra87]. Because this verification only adds local computation and piggybacked information to the consensus, it does not impact its correctness [CGLR18].

Let us first recall that the reliable broadcast protocol [Bra87] consists of the following steps. First a proposer broadcasts an init message containing a proposal. Upon reception, the proposal is then broadcast to all nodes in an echo message. (Note that the init message of the proposer is considered as its echo message.) Upon reception of $\lceil \frac{n+f+1}{2} \rceil$ equal echo messages, a ready message containing the proposal is broadcast. Upon reception of $2f + 1$ equal ready messages the proposal is delivered. If the node receives $f + 1$ equal ready messages before it has sent a ready message, it broadcasts that ready message without waiting.

Our verified variant of the reliable broadcast reduces the communication footprint by exchanging hashes $h(v)$ instead of the values v themselves when possible. It also adds a verification before the broadcast of the READY message. Namely, upon reception of $\lceil \frac{n+f+1}{2} \rceil$ equal ECHO messages at a verifier node, the verification of the proposal starts. Upon completion, a list of integers indicating the indices of invalid transactions in the proposal is appended to the READY message, which is then broadcast. Nodes that are not in the verifier sets will only broadcast a READY message upon the reception of $f + 1$ equal READY messages.

6.6.4.3 Reconciliation

Thanks to the verified reliable broadcast, each correct node ends up with an array of verified proposals and a bitmask, which is the array of n binary values corresponding to the binary consensus decisions. Although the array of verified proposals may differ across correct nodes, the bitmasks of all correct nodes are guaranteed to contains 1s and be identical due to the agreement properties of the binary consensus [CGLR18]. Correct nodes apply this bitmask to the array of proposals to obtain the indices of the proposals array at which the verified proposals are potentially decidable. Note that even though the proposal may not be known yet for some of these indices, it is guaranteed to be eventually known, thanks to the eventual delivery of

---

Algorithm 10 Verified reliable broadcast

1: verified-reliable-broadcast(v):
2:     broadcast(INIT, v)

3: **upon** receiving a message (INIT, v) from p_j:
4:     broadcast(ECHO, $h(v), j$)

5: **upon** receiving $n - f$ (ECHO, $h(v), j$) msgs and not having sent READY:
6:     **if** $p_i \in$ *primary_verifiers*(v) **then** *verif* $\leftarrow$ verify(v)
7:     **if** $p_i \in$ *secondary_verifiers*(v) **then** wait(Δ); *verif* $\leftarrow$ verify(v)
8:     broadcast(READY, *verif*, $h(v), j$)

9: **upon** receiving $f + 1$ (READY, *verif*, $h(v), j$) and not having sent READY:
10:     stop-verify(v)
11:     broadcast(READY, *verif*, $h(v), j$)

12: **upon** receiving $n - f$ (READY, *verif*, $h(v), j$) and not delivered from j:
13:     **if** is-verified(v, *verif*) **then** deliver(v, j)

---

the verifiable reliable broadcast that is identical at all correct nodes (cf. Section 6.6.4.2).

Each correct node waits until a potentially decidable proposal has been delivered at each of these indices, at which point they are guaranteed to have the exact same set of proposals. Then they extract the transactions that do not conflict from all these proposals. This extraction is done deterministically at all correct nodes by going through all proposals in increasing index number and through each of their transactions one-by-one, adding a transaction to the superblock if the UTXO it consumes exists, or simply discarding the transaction, if it conflicts (i.e., consumes the same UTXO) of an already selected transaction. For the sake of fairness (i.e., to not favor any particular proposer), correct nodes traverse the proposals from the index number ($k \bmod n$) to index number ($k - 1 \bmod n$) where k is the index of the latest superblock in the blockchain. This prevents the proposer with the lowest index number from having its proposed transactions added to the superblock with a higher priority than the transactions of other proposers.

Algorithm 11 Reconciliation

1: reconciliate(*props*):
2:     **for** $\ell = 0..(n - 1)$ **do**
3:         **for** $tx \in props[(k + \ell) \bmod n]$ **do**
4:             **for** $ctx \in$ *superblock* **do**
5:                 **if** $\neg$conflict(tx, ctx) **then** *superblock* $\leftarrow$ *superblock* $\cup \{tx\}$
6:     decide(*superblock*)

6.6.5 Binary Byzantine consensus of RBBC

To solve the binary consensus deterministically, we chose the binary consensus of DBFT [CGLR18] because it is resilience optimal and time optimal. DBFT is depicted in Algorithm 12 and is very similar to the safe variant we presented in Algorithm 8: it also builds upon the binary-value broadcast of Algorithm 8 but is simplified (we do not use the index i when clear from the context and round number r is assumed to start at 1), makes use of timers (lines 4 and 8) and a weak coordinator (lines 5–7) to help correct processes converge towards the same decision. In addition, each correct process that decides also executes two additional iterations of the loop (without re-deciding) to help undecided processes converge to their decisions (line 20).

Each replica refines an estimate value, now calleds *val*, initially its input value to the consensus, across consecutive rounds, starting from round $r = 1$, until it decides (line 14). It invokes broadcast primitives that deliver some values into a dedicated variable pointed out by $\rightarrow$ at lines 6, 7 and 10. The bv-broadcast (line 6) is a reliable broadcast for binary values [MMR15b]. (We optimize by piggybacking it for $r = 1$ with the verified-reliable-broadcast at line 2, this is the reason why we put the parentheses around the first broadcast invocation.) One replica per round acts as a coordinator by broadcasting its value c (line 7) that others prioritize (line 9) to help them converge to the same decision. Hence, RBBC is leaderless with multiple coordinators. The binary values are then forwarded in AUX messages (line 10) and each replica waits to receive a sufficiently represented set of these AUX values (lines 9–11). If only one value is sufficiently represented (line 12) and if it corresponds to the parity of the round, then it is decided (line 14). Otherwise, *val* is set to the parity of the round and another round starts.

6.6.6 Proof of Correctness

We show that our verified reliable broadcast ensures the properties of the reliable broadcast for valid values and discards invalid values, then we prove that our consensus protocol solves the Set Byzantine Consensus problem before showing that RBBC implements a replicated state machine (RSM).

Theorem 6.3. *The Verified Reliable Broadcast (lines 1–13) ensures the properties of the Reliable Broadcast for all valid values and does not deliver an invalid value at any correct proposer.*

Proof. We proceed by showing the properties of reliable broadcast for a valid value: if a valid value is delivered then it was broadcast (validity), a correct proposer delivers at most one value from any given proposer (unicity), if a correct proposer broadcasts a valid value v then v is delivered at all correct

Algorithm 12 The binary Byzantine consensus algorithm

```
 1: bin-propose(val):
 2:    repeat:
 3:        (bv-broadcast(EST, r, val) → bin-values)
 4:        start-timer(r)
 5:        if i = r mod n then
 6:            wait until (bin-values = {w})
 7:            broadcast(COORD, r, w) → c
 8:        wait until (bin-values ≠ ∅ ∧ timer expired)
 9:        if c ∈ bin-values then e ← {c} else e ← bin-values
10:        broadcast(AUX, r, e) → bvals
11:        wait until ∃s ⊆ bvals where the two following conditions hold:
12:            • if v received in AUX msgs of n − f processes then v ∈ s
13:            • ∀v ∈ s, v ∈ bin-values
14:        if s = {v} then
15:            val ← v
16:            if v = (r mod 2) and not decided yet then decide(v)
17:        else val ← (r mod 2)
18:        if decided in round r − 2 then exit()
19:        r ← r + 1
20:    until r is such that decide was invoked in round r − 2
```

proposers (termination1) and if a correct proposer delivers a valid value v, then all correct proposers deliver v (termination2). It is easy to ensure validity and unicity, so let us focus on termination1 and termination2. Consider that a valid value v is broadcast by some proposer p_i. There are two cases to consider, either p_i is correct or Byzantine.

1. **Proposer p_i is correct.** Proposer p_i broadcasts INIT to all proposers, hence each proposer broadcasts ECHO to all proposers, and all correct proposers eventually receive ECHO messages with v from $n - f$ distinct correct proposers. These correct proposers, say Q, are thus ready to start verifying value v. As there are $f + 1$ primary verifiers and f secondary verifiers, there are up to $2f + 1$ verifiers, say Q', that will verify value v if not stopped at line 10. If $f + 1$ verifiers broadcast READY messages with the same verification outcome $verif$, then we know that all correct proposers will then retransmit READY with this $verif$, which will guarantee that all correct proposers will receive $n - f$ messages $\langle$READY, $verif$, $h(v)$, $p_i \rangle$ and will thus deliver v (line 13). It thus remains to show that $f + 1$ verifiers will eventually broadcast READY messages with the same verification outcome $verif$. Note that $|Q \cap Q'| \geq f + 1$, which means that among the correct proposers Q, $f + 1$ of them verify v and obtain the same verification outcome $verif$ that they broadcast.

2. **Proposer p_i is Byzantine.** First, if proposer p_i broadcasts INIT successfully to all $n - t$ correct proposers, in which case, they all broadcast ECHO with value v to all proposers and the case is identical to case (1), where all cor-

rect proposers deliver v (line 13). In the case where proposer p_i does not broadcasts INIT to $f + 1$ correct proposers because it broadcasts to less proposers, then not enough proposers will receive INIT for ECHO to be received by sufficiently many proposers at line 5 and v will not be delivered. Third, if proposer p_i broadcasts INIT to $f + 1 \le \ell < n - f$ proposers, then it depends on the behaviors of the other Byzantine proposers, if sufficiently many of them send ECHO messages to $f + 1$ verifiers or if they help verifying correctly, then v will be delivered at all correct proposers, otherwise, it will not be delivered at any correct proposer.

To show that no invalid values can be delivered at any correct proposer, consider that v is invalid so there cannot be $f + 1$ distinct verifiers whose *verif* is identifying v as valid. As a result, if line 9 is enabled with $f + 1$ identical messages $\langle \text{READY}, verif, h(v), p_i \rangle$ from distinct proposers then we know that *verif* is necessarily identifying v as invalid and the precondition to deliver v at line 13 will not be satisfied.

Lemma 6.3. *In the binary Byzantine consensus (lines 4–15), if at the beginning of a round r, all correct proposers have the same estimate val, they never change their estimate value thereafter.*

Proof. Let us assume that all correct processes (which are at least $n - f > f + 1$) have the same estimate *val* when they start round r. Hence, they all bv-broadcast the same message EST(val) either at line 2 or within the reliable broadcast at line 6. It follows from the properties of the reliable broadcast [Bra87] and bv-broadcast [MMR15b] that each correct process p_i is such that $bin\text{-}values_i = \{v\}$ at line 9, and consequently can broadcast only ECHO($\{v\}$) at line 10. Considering any correct process p_i, it then follows from the predicate of line 11 (s_i contains only v), the predicate of line 12 (s_i is a singleton), and the assignment of line 14, that val_i keeps the value v.

The next lemma states that if the value s in the same round of two correct replicas are singletons then they are identical.

Lemma 6.4. *Let p_i and p_j be two correct proposers. In the Byzantine binary consensus (lines 4–15), if $s_i = \{v\}$ and $s_j = \{w\}$ in the same round, then $v = w$.*

Proof. Let p_i be a correct proposer such that $s_i = \{v\}$. It follows from line 11 that p_i received the same message AUX ($\{v\}$) from $(n - t)$ different processes, i.e., from at least $(n - 2f)$ different correct processes. As $n - 2t \ge f + 1$, this means that p_i received the message AUX ($\{v\}$) from a set Q_i including at least $(f + 1)$ different correct proposers.

Let p_j be a correct proposer such that $s_j = \{w\}$. Hence, p_j received AUX ($\{w\}$) from a set Q_j of at least $(n - t)$ different proposers. As $(n - f) + (f + 1) > n$, it follows that $Q_i \cap Q_j \ne \emptyset$. Let $p_k \in Q_i \cap Q_j$. As $p_k \in Q_i$, it is a correct proposer. Hence, at line 10, p_k sent the same AUX message to p_i and p_j, and we consequently have $v = w$.

Lemma 6.5 (Binary Consensus Validity). *In the Byzantine binary consensus (lines 4–15), the value decided by a correct proposer was proposed by a correct proposer.*

Proof. Let us consider the round $r = 1$. Due to the property of the bv-broadcast executed at line 2 or piggybacked within the reliable broadcast at line 6, it follows that the sets *bin-values$_i$* contains only values proposed by correct proposers. Consequently, the correct proposers broadcast, at line 10 AUX messages containing sets with values proposed only by correct proposers. It then follows from the predicate of line 11 ($s_i \subseteq$ *bin-values$_i$*), and the reliable and bv-broadcast properties, that the set s_i of each correct proposer contains only values proposed by correct proposers. Hence, the assignment of *val$_i$* (be it at line 13 or 15) provides it with a value proposed by a correct proposer. The same reasoning applies to rounds $r = 2$, $r = 3$, etc., which concludes the proof of the lemma.

Lemma 6.6 (Binary Consensus Agreement). *In the Byzantine binary consensus (lines 4–15), no two correct replicas decide different values.*

Proof. Let r be the first round during which a correct proposer decides, let p_i be a correct proposer that decides in round r (line 14), and let v be the value it decides. Hence, we have $s_i^r = \{v\}$ where $v = (r \bmod 2)$.

If another correct replica p_j decides during round r, we have $s_j^r = \{w\}$, and, due to Lemma 6.4, we have $w = v$. Hence, all correct proposers that decide in round r, decide v. Moreover, each correct proposer that decides in round r has previously assigned $v = (r \bmod 2)$ to its local estimate s_i.

Let p_j be a correct proposer that does not decide in round r. As $s_i^r = \{v\}$, and p_j does not decide in round r, it follows from Lemma 6.4 that we cannot have $s_j^r = \{1 - v\}$, and consequently $s_j^r = \{0, 1\}$. Hence, in round r, p_j executes line 13, where it assigns the value $(r \bmod 2) = v$ to its local estimate val_j.

It follows that all correct proposers start round $(r + 1)$ with the same local estimate $v = r \bmod 2$. Due to Lemma 6.3, they keep this estimate value forever. Hence, no different value can be decided in a future round by a correct proposer that has not decided during round r, which concludes the proof of the lemma.

Lemma 6.7. *During the RBBC consensus (lines 1–10) execution, at least one binary consensus instance decides 1.*

Proof. By Theorem 6.3, we know that all correct proposers eventually populate their proposal array with at least one common values. Due to the reduction, all correct proposers will thus have input 1 for the corresponding binary consensus instance. By the validity (Lemma 6.5) and termination [CGLR17] properties of the binary consensus, the decided value for this binary consensus instance has to be 1.

Lemma 6.8. *If a Byzantine binary consensus instance at index i decides 1, then the verified reliable broadcast (lines 1–13) at index i reliably delivers a value at a correct proposer.*

Proof. A correct proposer does not propose 1 to a binary consensus instance at index i without reliably delivering a proposal at index i. The result follows from Theorem 6.3 and the validity of the binary consensus (Lemma 6.5).

Theorem 6.4 (Set Byzantine Consensus). *The RBBC consensus (lines 1–10) solves the Set Byzantine Consensus.*

Proof. By Lemma 6.7, at one indice, a binary consensus instance terminates with 1. By Lemma 6.6, we know that all correct proposers have set 1 to the same indices of their *bitmask*. For each of these indices k there is a proposal *props*[k] that will be delivered at every correct proposer by Lemma 6.8. As a result, all correct proposers invoke function reconciliate with the same argument at line 10. By examination of the code at lines 1–6, all correct proposers thus put in their *superblock* the same subset of valid and non-conflicting transactions hence guaranteeing agreement, termination and validity of the SBC problem (Section 6.4).

Theorem 6.5 (Replicated State Machine). *The set of committed transactions of RBBC is totally ordered.*

Proof. In RBBC, all permissioned nodes run the consensus algorithm either because they receive messages from proposers or because they propose themselves. Each node starts by running a single instance of this consensus algorithm for the block at index 1 (after the genesis block). A node can start a new consensus instance for a block at index $j > 1$ only after the consensus instance at index $j - 1$ has terminated. As Theorem 6.4 shows that consensus guarantees agreement there is a single block decided per index of the blockchain. It results that blocks are totally ordered through their index number: whenever a block is decided, it is ordered after all previously decided blocks. Given that in each block the transactions do not conflict and are ordered through the same deterministic strategy employed by all correct nodes (lines 1–6), transactions are totally ordered.

6.7 Conclusion

Classic solutions to the problem of consensus predate the blockchain era. Most of these solutions rely on a leader-based design that induces some overhead when propagating a proposal to a large network. In order to scale blockchain technologies, one has to rethink their consensus components

Blockchain	deployment	network	throughput	latency	#nodes	#machines
Elastico [LNZ$^+$16]	country-wide	emulated	20 KB/s	800 sec	1,600	800
Algorand [GHM$^+$17]	country-wide	emulated	208 KB/s	12 sec	50,000	1000
Omniledger [KKJG$^+$17b]	datacenter	emulated	1.7 MB/s	14 sec	1,800	60
RapidChain [ZMR18]	datacenter	emulated	3.6 MB/s	9 sec	4,000	32
RBBC	world-wide	real	11.7 MB/s	3 sec	9,400	1000

Table 6.1 Scalable blockchain experiments – the throughput of Elastico, Omniledger and RapidChain was previously observed to be 40 TPS, 3500 TPS and 7380 TPS for 512-byte transactions [ZMR18], the throughput of Algorand was reported to be 750 MB/h=208 KB/s [GHM$^+$17], the throughput of RBBC is obtained from 30,684 TPS for 400-byte transactions [CNG18].

rather than reusing off-the-shelf solutions. However, the consensus problem is quite challenging, which led researchers to try to shard the consensus: running multiple consensus instances among fewer nodes in parallel.

Red Belly Blockchain takes a different approach by offering a solution that scales to hundreds of consensus nodes by leveraging a leaderless consensus design and verification sharding. Its consensus, called Democratic BFT, has been designed for blockchains. Red Belly Blockchain adapted this algorithm to combine multiple proposals from different nodes into a superblock without the need of a special leader node. The performance obtained is compared to alternative approaches, including sharding ones, in Table 6.1.

6.8 Bibliographic notes

The Democratic Byzantine Fault Tolerant (DBFT) consensus algorithm was originally presented in [CGLR18] and formally verified in [BGL$^+$22], and Red Belly Blockchain has been presented in [CNG21] and also evaluated in [CNG18] and [SNG20]. A version of Red Belly Blockchain supporting accountability was presented in [RPG20] and a version executing smart contracts written in Solidity was presented in [THG22]. This latter paper explains how to reduce the number of transaction validations to make smart contract execution scale with the number of validators.

Various layer-2 protocols were designed to bypass the scalability limitations of classic blockchains. Offchain protocols include state and payment channels [PD16, DW15, KGF18, MBKM17], and factories [BDW18]; some of which work without synchrony [AKW18, LNE$^+$18]. Sidechain or childchain protocols [BCD$^+$14, PB17, GKZ19] process transactions faster than the main chain. Crosschain swaps or deals [Nol16, Her18, ZHL$^+$18, ZAA19, HLS19, RPG19, vGGT20] exchange assets across blockchains.

Most partially synchronous Byzantine consensus solutions are leader-based [CL02, KAD+07, CMSK07, VCB+09, MJM09, AGK+15b, BSA14, YMR+19]. Some tentatives tried to solve the Byzantine consensus without a leader, however, these are either not detailed [Lam11] or experience exponential complexity [BS10]. To bypass the limitation of these approaches, the idea has been to run multiple instances in parallel, a technique called *sharding*. Elastico [LNZ+16], Omniledger [KKJG+18], RapidChain [ZMR18] and Monoxide [WW19] are examples of sharded blockchains. Sharding does not remedy the problem of having to order cross-shard transactions. In particular, Monoxide does not offer atomic cross-shard transactions.

The traditional consensus definition unnecessarily limits the scalability of the blockchain [Vuk16, Buc16, SBV18]: most blockchains decide at most one of the proposed blocks [Buc16, SBV18]. The scalability problem is even exacerbated with *batching*, the act of waiting to gather more than one transaction requests to send a block containing multiple transactions. The leader bottleneck effect has been observed empirically multiple times [HKJR10, GBFS16, VG19b].

To decide a superblock that combines all proposed blocks, one may think of solving a variant of the consensus problem to instead combine proposals, sent across disjoint communication links, into a decision [BOKR94, NCV05, CGLR17]. For example, the related problems of Agreement on a Core Set or Asynchronous Common Subset (ACS) [BOKR94], Interactive Consistency (IC) [LSP82] and Vector Consensus (VC) [NCV05] all require at least $f + 1$ (either $n - f$ or $f + 1$ with $n > 3f$) proposed values to be decided. In blockchain, however, there may not even be $f + 1$ compatible proposed blocks. SBC-Validity is inspired by the external validity property [CKPS01] that requires a decision to be valid and the idea of deciding at least $f + 1$ proposed values [LSP82, BOKR94], however, SBC-Validity cannot result from any combination of these properties. The full hand-written liveness proof of DBFT can be found in [CGLR17] and the model checked linear time logic version of it can be found in [BGL+22].

6.9 Exercises

Question 1

Mulitple correct answers. By assuming partial synchrony:

a. every message takes more than a bounded amount of time to reach their destination.
b. every message takes less than a bounded amount of time to reach their destination.
c. algorithm knows the bond on the amount of time.
d. algorithm does not know the bond on the amount of time.

Question 2

A well-known Byzantine consensus solution is called PBFT. What does the 'P' in PBFT stand for?

a. Practical
b. Partial
c. Pragmatic
d. Popular

Question 3

The misbehavior of a single node can slow down the performance of PBFT, which role does this node play?

a. The leader
b. The backup
c. The follower

Question 4

Regarding leader-led algorithms like PBFT, which of the following is *not* correct?

a. The process that plays the role of the leader is permanent
b. It is hard for the client to know whether the leader is misbehaving
b. The set of transactions is proposed by the leader

Question 5

For a client or wallet application, it is easier to identify and send requests to whom?

a. The process who is the leader
b. The processes that will run the consensus

Question 6

At large scale, the time to exchange sets of transactions is typically faster for what kind of consensus algorithms?

a. Leader-based
b. Leaderless

Question 7

The time it takes for all processes to be aware of the set of transactions is the same for both leader-based and leaderless algorithms in what kind of network?

a. Small
b. Large

Question 8

Consensus may not scale in a leader-based algorithm for various reasons. One reason is because consensus here does not leverage all the links. What does this mean?

a. The decided block must be proposed by the leader
b. The decided block has to be proposed by a non-leader process

Question 9

As we learned in this course, if consensus was reached by letting a leader impose its block proposals to other processes, the set of committed trans-actions would not scale with the amount of participants. Thus, the key to scalability in this situation is to decide a block that grows with the number of participants in the consensus. Which of the following is characteristics of this scalable consensus?

a. The decided block has to be a block proposed by one node
b. The decided block has to be the block proposed by the leader
c. The decided block can contain transactions proposed by different nodes

Question 10

Why does the Set Byzantine Consensus accept potentially valid transactions proposed by malicious nodes?

a. Because, as they are valid, these transactions only withdraw from the account of malicious nodes anyway
b. Because this consensus is designed for non-critical applications where malicious nodes can sometimes steal the assets of other nodes.

Question 11

In Set Byzantine Consensus, which of the three properties of consensus are different from previous Byzantine consensus definition?

a. Agreement
b. Termination
c. Validation

Question 12

What does the D in DBFT stand for?

a. Democratic
b. Divergent
c. Dual

Question 13

True or false? DBFT is called "Democratic" because no misbehaving leader can force the protocol to slow down.

Question 14

True or false? DBFT invokes multiple instances of a binary Byzantine consensus, each taking few message delays to terminate. These instances cannot run concurrently for DBFT to terminate quickly.

Question 15

Red Belly Blockchain is described as a community blockchain. What makes it different from consortium blockchains?

a. The set of validators and consensus participants are pre-determined
b. The set of validators and consensus participants change at runtime.

Question 16

Red Belly Blockchain is described as a community blockchain. What makes it different from public blockchains?

a. The system incentivizes all participants to mine the same blocks
b. The system does not incentivize all participants to mine the same blocks

Question 16

Red Belly Blockchain uses verification sharding to ensure that:

a. The storage resource of the processes is not wasted
b. The CPU resource of the processes is not wasted
c. The bandwidth of the processes is not wasted

Question 17

In Red Belly Blockchain, as more nodes join the set of participants, what generally happens to performance?

a. It increases
b. It decreases

Question 18

What is the asymptotic message complexity of the safe and live binary Byzantine consensus algorithm? What is the asymptotic message complexity of the DBFT consensus algorithm?

Question 19

What is the asymptotic communication complexity of the safe and live binary Byzantine consensus algorithm? What is the asymptotic communication complexity of the DBFT consensus algorithm?

Question 20

What is the asymptotic time complexity of the safe and live binary Byzantine consensus algorithm? What is the asymptotic time complexity of the DBFT consensus algorithm?

Question 21

Let m be the number of transactions proposed to the Set Byzantine Consensus by each proposer of Red Belly Blockchain and let n be the number of proposers. Assume that all transactions are correctly signed and that correct proposals are all reliably delivered before the algorithm times out (line 4) but that all $\lceil \frac{n}{3} \rceil - 1$ Byzantine proposers do not propose any transaction.

a. What is the minimum number of transactions, depending on m, that Red Belly Blockchain commits if all the duplicated transactions of requesters are proposed to the same consensus instance?
b. What is the number of transactions that Red Belly Blockchain commits if each requester transaction is sent to one correct proposer and the f Byzantine proposers?

References

AGK+15.   Pierre-Louis Aublin, Rachid Guerraoui, Nikola Knežević, Vivien Quéma, and Marko Vukolić. The next 700 BFT protocols. *ACM Trans. Comput. Syst.*, 32(4):12:1–12:45, January 2015.

AKW18.   Georgia Avarikioti, Eleftherios Kokoris Kogias, and Roger Wattenhofer. Brick: Asynchronous state channels. Technical Report 1905.11360, arXiv, 2018.

BCD+14.   Adam Back, Matt Corallo, Luke Dashjr, Mark Friedenbach, Gregory Maxwell, Andrew Miller, Andrew Poelstra, Jorge Timón, and Pieter Wuille. Enabling blockchain innovations with pegged sidechains. *URL: http://www. opensciencereview. com/papers/123/enablingblockchain-innovations-with-pegged-sidechains*, page 72, 2014.

BDW18.   Conrad Burchert, Christian Decker, and Roger Wattenhofer. Scalable funding of bitcoin micropayment channel networks. *Royal Society open science*, 5(8):180089, 2018.

BGL+22.   Nathalie Bertrand, Vincent Gramoli, Marijana Lazić, Igor Konnov, Pierre Tholoniat, and Josef Widder. Brief announcement: Holistic verification of blockchain consensus. In *Proceedings of the ACM Symposium on Distributed Computing (PODC)*, 2022.

BOKR94.   Michael Ben-Or, Boaz Kelmer, and Tal Rabin. Asynchronous secure computations with optimal resilience (extended abstract). In *Proceedings of the Thirteenth Annual ACM Symposium on Principles of Distributed Computing*, PODC '94, pages 183–192, New York, NY, USA, 1994. ACM.

Bra87.   Gabriel Bracha. Asynchronous byzantine agreement protocols. *Inf. Comput.*, 75(2):130–143, November 1987.

BS10.   Fatemeh Borran and André Schiper. A leader-free byzantine consensus algorithm. In Krishna Kant, Sriram V. Pemmaraju, Krishna M. Sivalingam, and Jie Wu, editors, *Distributed Computing and Networking*, pages 67–78, Berlin, Heidelberg, 2010. Springer Berlin Heidelberg.

BSA14.   Alyson Bessani, Joao Sousa, and Eduardo E. P. Alchieri. State machine replication for the masses with BFT-SMaRt. In *2014 44th Annual IEEE/IFIP International Conference on Dependable Systems and Networks*, pages 355–362, June 2014.

Buc16.   Ethan Buchman. Tendermint: Byzantine fault tolerance in the age of blockchains, 2016. MS Thesis.

CCCG20.   Christian Cachin, Daniel Collins, Tyler Crain, and Vincent Gramoli. Anonymity preserving byzantine vector consensus. In *European Symposium on Research in Computer Security (ESORICS)*, pages 133–152. Springer International Publishing, 2020.

CGLR17.   Tyler Crain, Vincent Gramoli, Mikel Larrea, and Michel Raynal. (leader/randomization/signature)-free byzantine consensus for consortium blockchains. Technical report, arXiv, 2017.

CGLR18.   Tyler Crain, Vincent Gramoli, Mikel Larrea, and Michel Raynal. DBFT: Efficient leaderless byzantine consensus and its applications to blockchains. In *Proceedings of the 17th IEEE International Symposium on Network Computing and Applications (NCA'18)*, 2018.

CKPS01.   Christian Cachin, Klaus Kursawe, Frank Petzold, and Victor Shoup. Secure and efficient asynchronous broadcast protocols. In *Proceedings of the 21st Annual International Cryptology Conference on Advances in Cryptology*, CRYPTO '01, pages 524–541, London, UK, UK, 2001. Springer-Verlag.

CL02.   Miguel Castro and Barbara Liskov. Practical byzantine fault tolerance and proactive recovery. *ACM Trans. Comput. Syst.*, 20(4):398–461, 2002.

CMSK07.   Byung-Gon Chun, Petros Maniatis, Scott Shenker, and John Kubiatowicz. Attested append-only memory: Making adversaries stick to their word. In *Pro-*

ceedings of Twenty-first ACM SIGOPS Symposium on Operating Systems Principles, SOSP '07, pages 189–204, New York, NY, USA, 2007. ACM.

CNG18.   Tyler Crain, Christopher Natoli, and Vincent Gramoli. Evaluating the red belly blockchain. Technical Report 1812.11747, arXiv, 2018.

CNG21.   Tyler Crain, Christopher Natoli, and Vincent Gramoli. Red belly: A secure, fair and scalable open blockchain. In *Proceedings of the 42nd IEEE Symposium on Security and Privacy (SP'21)*, pages 466–483. IEEE, 2021.

DW15.   Christian Decker and Roger Wattenhofer. A fast and scalable payment network with bitcoin duplex micropayment channels. In *Symposium on Self-Stabilizing Systems*, pages 3–18. Springer, 2015.

GBFS16.   Vincent Gramoli, Len Bass, Alan Fekete, and Daniel Sun. Rollup: Non-disruptive rolling upgrade with fast consensus-based dynamic reconfigurations. *IEEE Transactions on Parallel and Distributed Systems (TPDS)*, 27(9):2711–2724, Sep 2016.

GHM+17.   Yossi Gilad, Rotem Hemo, Silvio Micali, Georgios Vlachos, and Nickolai Zeldovich. Algorand: Scaling byzantine agreements for cryptocurrencies. In *Proceedings of the 26th Symposium on Operating Systems Principles*, SOSP '17, pages 51–68, 2017.

GKZ19.   Peter Gazi, Aggelos Kiayias, and Dionysis Zindros. Proof-of-stake sidechains. In *IEEE Symposium on Security & Privacy*, 2019.

Her18.   Maurice Herlihy. Atomic cross-chain swaps. In *Proceedings of the 2018 ACM Symposium on Principles of Distributed Computing*, pages 245–254. ACM, 2018.

HKJR10.   Patrick Hunt, Mahadev Konar, Flavio P. Junqueira, and Benjamin Reed. Zookeeper: Wait-free coordination for internet-scale systems. In *ATC*, pages 11–11. USENIX, 2010.

HLS19.   Maurice Herlihy, Barbara Liskov, and Liuba Shrira. Cross-chain deals and adversarial commerce. *Proc. VLDB Endow.*, 13:100–113, October 2019.

KAD+07.   Ramakrishna Kotla, Lorenzo Alvisi, Mike Dahlin, Allen Clement, and Edmund Wong. Zyzzyva: Speculative byzantine fault tolerance. In *Proceedings of Twenty-first ACM SIGOPS Symposium on Operating Systems Principles*, SOSP '07, pages 45–58, New York, NY, USA, 2007. ACM.

KGF18.   Rami Khalil, Arthur Gervais, and Guillaume Felley. NOCUST–a securely scalable commit-chain. Technical Report 642, Cryptology ePrint Archive, 2018.

KKJG+17.   Eleftherios Kokoris-Kogias, Philipp Jovanovic, Linus Gasser, Nicolas Gailly, Ewa Syta, and Bryan Ford. Omniledger: A secure, scale-out, decentralized ledger via sharding. Cryptology ePrint Archive, Report 2017/406, 2017. http s://eprint.iacr.org/2017/406.

KKJG+18.   Eleftherios Kokoris-Kogias, Philipp Jovanovic, Linus Gasser, Nicolas Gailly, Ewa Syta, and Bryan Ford. Omniledger: A secure, scale-out, decentralized ledger via sharding. In *2018 IEEE Symposium on Security and Privacy (SP)*, pages 583–598, 2018.

Lam11.   Leslie Lamport. Brief announcement: Leaderless byzantine paxos. In *Distributed Computing - 25th International Symposium, DISC 2011, Rome, Italy, September 20-22, 2011. Proceedings*, pages 141–142, 2011.

LNE+18.   Joshua Lind, Oded Naor, Ittay Eyal, Florian Kelbert, Peter Pietzuch, and Emin Gün Sirer. Teechain: Reducing storage costs on the blockchain with offline payment channels. In *Proceedings of the 11th ACM International Systems and Storage Conference*, pages 125–125. ACM, 2018.

LNZ+16.   Loi Luu, Viswesh Narayanan, Chaodong Zheng, Kunal Baweja, Seth Gilbert, and Prateek Saxena. A secure sharding protocol for open blockchains. In *Proceedings of the 2016 ACM SIGSAC Conference on Computer and Communications Security*, CCS '16, pages 17–30, 2016.

LSP82.   Leslie Lamport, Robert Shostak, and Marshall Pease. The byzantine generals problem. *ACM Trans. Program. Lang. Syst.*, 4(3):382–401, July 1982.

MBKM17.   Andrew Miller, Iddo Bentov, Ranjit Kumaresan, and Patrick McCorry. Sprites: Payment channels that go faster than lightning. Technical Report 1702.05812, arXiv, 2017.

MJM09.   Yanhua Mao, Flavio P. Junqueira, and Keith Marzullo. Towards low latency state machine replication for uncivil wide-area networks. In *In Workshop on Hot Topics in System Dependability*, 2009.

MMR15.   Achour Mostéfaoui, Hamouma Moumen, and Michel Raynal. Signature-free asynchronous binary byzantine consensus with $T < N/3$, $O(N^2)$ messages, and $O(1)$ expected time. *J. ACM*, 62(4):31:1–31:21, September 2015.

Nak08.   Satoshi Nakamoto. Bitcoin: a peer-to-peer electronic cash system, 2008. http://www.bitcoin.org.

NCV05.   Nuno F. Neves, Miguel Correia, and Paulo Verissimo. Solving vector consensus with a wormhole. *IEEE Trans. Parallel Distrib. Syst.*, 16(12):1120–1131, December 2005.

Nol16.   Tier Nolan. Atomic swaps using cut and choose. https://bitcointalk.org/index.php?topic=1364951, 2016.

PB17.   Joseph Poon and Vitalik Buterin. Plasma: Scalable autonomous smart contracts. *White paper*, pages 1–47, 2017.

PD16.   Joseph Poon and Thaddeus Dryja. The bitcoin lightning network: Scalable off-chain instant payments, 2016.

RPG19.   Alejandro Ranchal-Pedrosa and Vincent Gramoli. Platypus: Offchain protocol without synchrony. In *Proceedings of the 18th IEEE International Symposium on Network Computing and Applications (NCA'19)*, pages 1–8. IEEE, Sep 2019.

RPG20.   Alejandro Ranchal-Pedrosa and Vincent Gramoli. Blockchain is dead, long live blockchain! Accountable state machine replication for longlasting blockchain. Technical Report 2007.10541, arXiv, 2020.

SBV18.   Joao Sousa, Alysson Bessani, and Marko Vukolić. A byzantine fault-tolerant ordering service for the hyperledger fabric blockchain platform. In *2018 48th Annual IEEE/IFIP International Conference on Dependable Systems and Networks (DSN)*, pages 51–58, June 2018.

SNG20.   Gary Shapiro, Christopher Natoli, and Vincent Gramoli. The performance of Byzantine fault tolerant blockchains. In *Proceedings of the 19th IEEE International Symposium on Network Computing and Applications (NCA'20)*. IEEE, Nov 2020.

THG22.   Deepal Tennakoon, Yiding Hua, and Vincent Gramoli. CollaChain: A BFT collaborative middleware for decentralized applications. Technical Report 2203.12323, arXiv, 2022.

VCB⁺09.   Giuliana Veronese, Miguel Correia, Alysson Bessani, Lau Cheuk Lung, and Paulo Verissimo. Minimal byzantine fault tolerance. Technical Report TR-2009-15, DI-FCUL, June 2009.

VG19a.   Guillaume Vizier and Vincent Gramoli. Comchain: A blockchain with Byzantine fault tolerant reconfiguration. *Concurrency and Computation, Practice and Experience*, 32(12), Oct 2019.

VG19b.   Gauthier Voron and Vincent Gramoli. Dispel: Byzantine SMR with distributed pipelining. Technical Report 1912.10367, arXiv, 2019.

vGGT20.   Rob van Glabbeek, Vincent Gramoli, and Pierre Tholoniat. Feasibility of cross-chain payment with success guarantees. In *Proceedings of the 32nd ACM Symposium on Parallelism in Algorithms and Architectures*, page 579?581, 2020.

Vuk16.   Marco Vukolíc. The quest for scalable blockchain fabric: Proof-of-work vs. BFT replication. In *Proceedings of the IFIP WG 11.4 Workshop on Open Research Problems in Network Security (iNetSec 2015)*, LNCS, pages 112–125, 2016.

WW19.   Jiaping Wang and Hao Wang. Monoxide: Scale out blockchains with asynchronous consensus zones. In *16th USENIX Symposium on Networked Systems Design and Implementation (NSDI 19)*, pages 95–112, Boston, MA, February 2019. USENIX Association.

YMR⁺19. Maofan Yin, Dahlia Malkhi, Michael K. Reiter, Guy Golan-Gueta, and Ittai Abraham. HotStuff: BFT consensus with linearity and responsiveness. In *Proceedings of the 2019 ACM Symposium on Principles of Distributed Computing*, pages 347–356, 2019.

ZAA19. Victor Zakhary, Divyakant Agrawal, and Amr El Abbadi. Atomic commitment across blockchains. Technical Report 1905.02847, arXiv, 2019.

ZHL⁺18. Alexei Zamyatin, Dominik Harz, Joshua Lind, Panayiotis Panayiotou, Arthur Gervais, and William J Knottenbelt. Xclaim: Interoperability with cryptocurrency-backed tokens. Technical Report 2018/643, Cryptology ePrint Archive, 2018.

ZMR18. Mahdi Zamani, Mahnush Movahedi, and Mariana Raykova. Rapidchain: Scaling blockchain via full sharding. Cryptology ePrint Archive, Report 2018/460, 2018. https://eprint.iacr.org/2018/460.

Chapter 7
Concluding Remarks

> The web is for everyone and collectively we hold the power to change it. It won't be easy. But if we dream a little and work a lot, we can get the web we want.
>
> *Sir Tim Berners-Lee*

© Springer Nature Switzerland AG 2022
V. Gramoli, *Blockchain Scalability and its Foundations in Distributed Systems*,
https://doi.org/10.1007/978-3-031-12578-2_7

By decentralizing the control over the data, blockchains offer a medium to empower end users in their economic interactions. The growing variety of transparent applications blockchains run offer as many options for users to interact with each other, without the need to trust the centralized, often opaque, alternative applications. As a drawback of this decentralization, blockchains are however often slower and more exposed to attacks than closed and centralized services. By helping computer scientists build new secure and scalable blockchains, this book aims at contributing towards the secure and efficient development of fairer services ideally suited for the sharing economy.

This is why this book has focused on the foundational concepts of the field of distributed computing and networking that affect the security and scalability of blockchain systems. Through running examples related to the classic blockchains, like Bitcoin and Ethereum, we have illustrated some of the resulting security limitations. We have then proposed classic consensus algorithms from the distributed computing literature to strengthen the security of these blockchains. Finally, through an analysis of these algorithms we presented the scalability limitations of more modern blockchain designs before presenting the Red Belly Blockchain as an alternative solution.

In particular, this book aimed at combining distributed computing foundational concepts and blockchain technologies, omitting distributed computing concepts that could be seen as less relevant to blockchains, like shared memory concepts. Other distributed computing books written by colleagues explore some of these foundational concepts in more depth.

- The book by Lynch [Lyn96] offers a specification of distributed algorithms in the Input/Output Automaton language.
- The book by Attiya and Welch [AW04] unifies shared memory and message passing algorithms.
- The book by Raynal on communication and agreement abstractions [Ray10] covers consensus algorithms for the asynchronous model.
- The book by Cachin, Guerraoui and Rodrigues [CGR11] presents distributed programming to tolerate both crashes and Byzantine failures.
- The book by Raynal on fault-tolerant message passing [Ray18] covers synchronous and asynchronous distributed algorithms tolerating crashes and Byzantine failures.

As blockchain spans various research fields, other books cover other parts of the blockchain topic. Some are dedicated to the blockchain developer, the science student or the software architect:

- The book by Narayanan, Bonneau, Felten, Miller and Goldfeder [NBF+16] presents Bitcoin with a detailed view of its internal implementation and discusses alternative coins.
- The book by Wattenhoffer [Wat16] covers a series of foundational consensus algorithms some of them could help make blockchain secure.

- The book by Shi [Shi] presents some foundations of distributed computing and probability theory and introduces Nakamoto's consensus algorithm.
- The book by Xu, Weber and Staples [XWS19] describes blockchain platforms and use-cases with a focus on software architecture.
- The book edited by Tran, Thai and Krishnamachari [TTK22] groups surveys and expository contributions on the state-of-the-art of blockchains.
- The book edited by Conti, Kanhere and Ruj [CKR22] covers theoretical foundations, platforms and applications of blockchains.

We hope this book has contributed to explain or clarify some misconceptions about the role of a consensus solution in a blockchain and what are the mistakes to avoid to build scalable blockchain systems for critical applications that cannot tolerate asset losses.

References

ABB⁺18.   Elli Androulaki, Artem Barger, Vita Bortnikov, Christian Cachin, Konstanti-
             nos Christidis, Angelo De Caro, David Enyeart, Christopher Ferris, Gen-
             nady Laventman, Yacov Manevich, Srinivasan Muralidharan, Chet Murthy,
             Binh Nguyen, Manish Sethi, Gari Singh, Keith Smith, Alessandro Sorniotti,
             Chrysoula Stathakopoulou, Marko Vukolić, Sharon Weed Cocco, and Jason
             Yellick. Hyperledger fabric: A distributed operating system for permissioned
             blockchains. In *Proceedings of the Thirteenth EuroSys Conference*, EuroSys '18,
             pages 30:1–30:15, 2018.
ADPL⁺19.   Emmanuelle Anceaume, Antonella Del Pozzo, Romaric Ludinard, Maria
             Potop-Butucaru, and Sara Tucci-Piergiovanni. Blockchain abstract data type.
             In *Proceedings of the 31st ACM Symposium on Parallelism in Algorithms and Ar-
             chitectures (SPAA)*, pages 349–358, 2019.
AGK⁺15a.   Pierre-Louis Aublin, Rachid Guerraoui, Nikola Knežević, Vivien Quéma,
             and Marko Vukolić. The next 700 BFT protocols. *ACM Trans. Comput. Syst.*,
             32(4):12:1–12:45, January 2015.
AGK⁺15b.   Pierre-Louis Aublin, Rachid Guerraoui, Nikola Knežević, Vivien Quéma,
             and Marko Vukolić. The next 700 BFT protocols. *ACM Trans. Comput. Syst.*,
             32(4):12:1–12:45, January 2015.
AKGN18.   Antonio Fernández Anta, Kishori Konwar, Chryssis Georgiou, and Nico-
             las Nicolaou. Formalizing and implementing distributed ledger objects.
             SIGACT News, 49(2):58–76, jun 2018.
AKW18.   Georgia Avarikioti, Eleftherios Kokoris Kogias, and Roger Wattenhofer.
             Brick: Asynchronous state channels. Technical Report 1905.11360, arXiv,
             2018.
AMN⁺17.   Ittai Abraham, Dahlia Malkhi, Kartik Nayak, Ling Ren, and Alexander
             Spiegelman. Solida: A blockchain protocol based on reconfigurable byzan-
             tine consensus. In *Proc. of the 21st International Conference on Principles of Dis-
             tributed Systems, (OPODIS)*, pages 25:1–25:19, 2017.
AW04.   Hagit Attiya and Jennifer Welch. *Distributed Computing. Fundamentals, Simu-
             lations, and Advanced Topics.* John Wiley & Sons, 2004.
AZV17.   Maria Apostolaki, Aviv Zohar, and Laurent Vanbever. Hijacking bitcoin:
             Routing attacks on cryptocurrencies. In *IEEE S&P 2017*, pages 375–392, 2017.
Bac02.   Adam Back. Hashcash - a denial of service counter-measure, 2002.
BCD⁺14.   Adam Back, Matt Corallo, Luke Dashjr, Mark Friedenbach, Gregory
             Maxwell, Andrew Miller, Andrew Poelstra, Jorge Timón, and Pieter
             Wuille. Enabling blockchain innovations with pegged sidechains. *URL:
             http://www. opensciencereview. com/papers/123/enablingblockchain-innovations-
             with-pegged-sidechains*, page 72, 2014.
BCGH16.   Richard Gendal Brown, James Carlyle, Ian Grigg, and Mike Hearn. Corda:
             An introduction, 2016.
BDDS92.   Amotz Bar-Noy, Danny Dolev, Cynthia Dwork, and H. Raymond Strong.
             Shifting gears: Changing algorithms on the fly to expedite byzantine agree-
             ment. *Inf. Comput.*, 97(2):205–233, 1992.
BDW18.   Conrad Burchert, Christian Decker, and Roger Wattenhofer. Scalable fund-
             ing of bitcoin micropayment channel networks. *Royal Society open science*,
             5(8):180089, 2018.
BGL⁺22.   Nathalie Bertrand, Vincent Gramoli, Marijana Lazić, Igor Konnov, Pierre
             Tholoniat, and Josef Widder. Brief announcement: Holistic verification of
             blockchain consensus. In *Proceedings of the ACM Symposium on Distributed
             Computing (PODC)*, 2022.
Bla02.   Adam Black. Hashcash - a denial of service counter-measure. Technical
             report, Cypherspace, 2002. http://www.hashcash.org/papers/hash
             cash.pdf.

BO83.   Michael Ben-Or. Another advantage of free choice (extended abstract): Completely asynchronous agreement protocols. In *Proceedings of the Second Annual ACM Symposium on Principles of Distributed Computing*, PODC '83, pages 27–30, 1983.

BOKR94.   Michael Ben-Or, Boaz Kelmer, and Tal Rabin. Asynchronous secure computations with optimal resilience (extended abstract). In *Proceedings of the Thirteenth Annual ACM Symposium on Principles of Distributed Computing*, PODC '94, pages 183–192, New York, NY, USA, 1994. ACM.

BPS16.   Iddo Bentov, Rafael Pass, and Elaine Shi. Snow white: Provably secure proofs of stake. Technical Report 919, IACR Cryptology ePrint Archive, 2016.

Bra87.   Gabriel Bracha. Asynchronous byzantine agreement protocols. *Inf. Comput.*, 75(2):130–143, November 1987.

BS10.   Fatemeh Borran and André Schiper. A leader-free byzantine consensus algorithm. In Krishna Kant, Sriram V. Pemmaraju, Krishna M. Sivalingam, and Jie Wu, editors, *Distributed Computing and Networking*, pages 67–78, Berlin, Heidelberg, 2010. Springer Berlin Heidelberg.

BSA14.   Alyson Bessani, Joao Sousa, and Eduardo E. P. Alchieri. State machine replication for the masses with BFT-SMaRt. In *2014 44th Annual IEEE/IFIP International Conference on Dependable Systems and Networks*, pages 355–362, June 2014.

BT83.   Gabriel Bracha and Sam Toueg. Asynchronous consensus and byzantine protocols in faulty environments. Technical Report TR83-559, Cornell University, 1983.

Buc16.   Ethan Buchman. Tendermint: Byzantine fault tolerance in the age of blockchains, 2016. MS Thesis.

But15.   Vitalik Buterin. On slow and fast block times, 9 2015. https://blog.ethereum.org/2015/09/14/on-slow-and-fast-block-times/.

But16a.   Vitalik Buterin. How should I handle blockchain forks in my DApp?, 1 2016. https://ethereum.stackexchange.com/questions/183/how-should-i-handle-blockchain-forks-in-my-dapp/203/#203.

But16b.   Vitalik Buterin. How should i handle blockchain forks in my dapp?, 1 2016. https://ethereum.stackexchange.com/questions/183/how-should-i-handle-blockchain-forks-in-my-dapp/203/#203.

Cac01.   Christian Cachin. Distributing trust on the internet. In *Proceedings of the International Conference on Dependable Systems and Networks (DSN)*, pages 183–192, 2001.

CAI.   CAIDA: Center for Applied Internet Data Analysis.

CAI17.   The CAIDA AS Relationships Dataset, August 2017.

CCCG20.   Christian Cachin, Daniel Collins, Tyler Crain, and Vincent Gramoli. Anonymity preserving byzantine vector consensus. In *European Symposium on Research in Computer Security (ESORICS)*, pages 133–152. Springer International Publishing, 2020.

CGG19.   Pierre Civit, Seth Gilbert, and Vincent Gramoli. Polygraph: Accountable byzantine consensus. In *Workshop on Verification of Distributed Systems (VDS'19)*, Jun 2019.

CGG21.   Pierre Civit, Seth Gilbert, and Vincent Gramoli. Polygraph: Accountable byzantine agreement. In *Proceedings of the 41st IEEE International Conference on Distributed Computing Systems (ICDCS)*, pages 403–413, 2021.

CGG⁺22a.   Pierre Civit, Seth Gilbert, Vincent Gramoli, Rachid Guerraoui, and Jovan Komatovic. As easy as ABC: Optimal (A)ccountable (B)yzantine (C)onsensus is easy! In *Proceedings of the 36th IEEE International Parallel and Distributed Processing Symposium (IPDPS'22)*. IEEE, 2022.

CGG⁺22b.   Pierre Civit, Seth Gilbert, Vincent Gramoli, Rachid Guerraoui, Jovan Komatovic, Zarko Milosevic, and Adi Serendinschi. Crime and punishment in distributed byzantine decision tasks. In *Proceedings of the 42nd IEEE International Conference on Distributed Computing Systems (ICDCS'22)*, 2022.

CGLR17.   Tyler Crain, Vincent Gramoli, Mikel Larrea, and Michel Raynal. (leader/randomization/signature)-free byzantine consensus for consortium blockchains. Technical report, arXiv, 2017.

CGLR18.   Tyler Crain, Vincent Gramoli, Mikel Larrea, and Michel Raynal. DBFT: Efficient leaderless byzantine consensus and its applications to blockchains. In *Proceedings of the 17th IEEE International Symposium on Network Computing and Applications (NCA'18)*, 2018.

CGR11.   Christian Cachin, Rachid Guerraoui, and Lus Rodrigues. *Introduction to Reliable and Secure Distributed Programming*. Springer Publishing Company, Incorporated, 2nd edition, 2011.

CHT96.   Tushar Deepak Chandra, Vassos Hadzilacos, and Sam Toueg. The weakest failure detector for solving consensus. *J. ACM*, 43(4):685–722, July 1996.

CKPS01.   Christian Cachin, Klaus Kursawe, Frank Petzold, and Victor Shoup. Secure and efficient asynchronous broadcast protocols. In *Proceedings of the 21st Annual International Cryptology Conference on Advances in Cryptology*, CRYPTO '01, pages 524–541, London, UK, UK, 2001. Springer-Verlag.

CKR22.   Mauro Conti, Salil Kanhere, and Sushmita Ruj. *Blockchains - A Handbook on Fundamentals, Platforms and Application*. Springer, 2022. To appear 2022.

CL02.   Miguel Castro and Barbara Liskov. Practical byzantine fault tolerance and proactive recovery. *ACM Trans. Comput. Syst.*, 20(4):398–461, 2002.

CMSK07.   Byung-Gon Chun, Petros Maniatis, Scott Shenker, and John Kubiatowicz. Attested append-only memory: Making adversaries stick to their word. In *Proceedings of Twenty-first ACM SIGOPS Symposium on Operating Systems Principles*, SOSP '07, pages 189–204, New York, NY, USA, 2007. ACM.

CNG18.   Tyler Crain, Christopher Natoli, and Vincent Gramoli. Evaluating the red belly blockchain. Technical Report 1812.11747, arXiv, 2018.

CNG21.   Tyler Crain, Christopher Natoli, and Vincent Gramoli. Red belly: A secure, fair and scalable open blockchain. In *Proceedings of the 42nd IEEE Symposium on Security and Privacy (SP'21)*, pages 466–483. IEEE, 2021.

CT96.   Tushar Deepak Chandra and Sam Toueg. Unreliable failure detectors for reliable distributed systems. *J. ACM*, 43(2):225–267, 1996.

Dav83.   Chaum David. Blind signatures for untraceable payments. *Advances in Cryptology*, 1983.

DB.   DB-IP - IP Geolocation and Network Intelligence. https://db-ip.com/.

DH76.   Whitfield Diffie and Martin Hellman. New directions in cryptography. *IEEE Transactions on Information Theory*, 22(6):644–654, 1976.

DLS88.   Cynthia Dwork, Nancy Lynch, and Larry Stockmeyer. Consensus in the presence of partial synchrony. *J. ACM*, 35(2):288–323, April 1988.

DN93.   Cynthia Dwork and Moni Naor. Pricing via processing or combatting junk mail. In *Advances in Cryptology (CRYPTO)*, volume 740 of *LNCS*. Springer, 1993.

DPS$^+$14.   Maya Dotan, Yvonne-Anne Pignolet, Stefan Schmid, Saar Tochner, and Aviv Zohar. Survey on cryptocurrency networking: Context, state-of-the-art, challenges. Technical Report 1409.6606, arXiv, 2014.

DW13.   Christian Decker and Roger Wattenhofer. Information propagation in the bitcoin network. In *Proc. of the IEEE International Conference on Peer-to-Peer Computing*, pages 1–10, 2013.

DW15.   Christian Decker and Roger Wattenhofer. A fast and scalable payment network with bitcoin duplex micropayment channels. In *Symposium on Self-Stabilizing Systems*, pages 3–18. Springer, 2015.

EGJ18.   Parinya Ekparinya, Vincent Gramoli, and Guillaume Jourjon. Impact of man-in-the-middle attacks on ethereum. In *SRDS*, 2018.

EGJ19.   Parinya Ekparinya, Vincent Gramoli, and Guillaume Jourjon. The attack of the clones against proof-of-authority. In *Community Ethereum Development Conference (EDCON'19)*, 2019.

EGJ20.   Parinya Ekparinya, Vincent Gramoli, and Guillaume Jourjon. The Attack
           of the Clones against Proof-of-Authority. In *Proceedings of the Network and
           Distributed Systems Security Symposium (NDSS'20)*. Internet Society, Feb 2020.

EGSvR16.   Ittay Eyal, Adem Efe Gencer, Emin Gün Sirer, and Robbert van Renesse.
           Bitcoin-NG: A scalable blockchain protocol. In *13th USENIX Symposium on
           Networked Systems Design and Implementation (NSDI)*, pages 45–59, 2016.

ES14.   Ittay Eyal and Emin Gün Sirer. Majority is not enough: Bitcoin mining is
           vulnerable. In *Financial Cryptography and Data Security - 18th International
           Conference, FC 2014, Christ Church, Barbados, March 3-7, 2014, Revised Selected
           Papers*, pages 436–454, 2014.

Fin11.   Hal Finney. Finney's attack, February 2011.

FLP85.   Michael J. Fischer, Nancy A. Lynch, and Michael S. Paterson. Impossibility of
           distributed consensus with one faulty process. *J. ACM*, 32(2):374–382, April
           1985.

GBFS16.   Vincent Gramoli, Len Bass, Alan Fekete, and Daniel Sun. Rollup: Non-
           disruptive rolling upgrade with fast consensus-based dynamic reconfigura-
           tions. *IEEE Transactions on Parallel and Distributed Systems (TPDS)*, 27(9):2711–
           2724, Sep 2016.

GHM+17.   Yossi Gilad, Rotem Hemo, Silvio Micali, Georgios Vlachos, and Nickolai Zel-
           dovich. Algorand: Scaling byzantine agreements for cryptocurrencies. In
           Proceedings of the 26th Symposium on Operating Systems Principles, SOSP '17,
           pages 51–68, 2017.

GKKT16.   J. Göbel, H.P. Keeler, A.E. Krzesinski, and P.G. Taylor. Bitcoin blockchain
           dynamics: The selfish-mine strategy in the presence of propagation delay.
           Performance Evaluation, Juy 2016.

GKL15.   Juan A. Garay, Aggelos Kiayias, and Nikos Leonardos. The bitcoin backbone
           protocol: Analysis and applications. In *Proceedings of the 34th Annual Inter-
           national Conference on the Theory and Applications of Cryptographic Technique
           (EUROCRYPT)*, pages 281–310, 2015.

GKM+19.   Rachid Guerraoui, Petr Kuznetsov, Matteo Monti, Matej Pavlovič, and
           Dragos-Adrian Seredinschi. The consensus number of a cryptocurrency. In
           Proceedings of the 2019 ACM Symposium on Principles of Distributed Computing,
           pages 307–316, 2019.

GKW+16.   Arthur Gervais, Ghassan O. Karame, Karl Wüst, Vasileios Glykantzis, Hu-
           bert Ritzdorf, and Srdjan Capkun. On the security and performance of proof
           of work blockchains. In *Proceedings of the 2016 ACM SIGSAC Conference on
           Computer and Communications Security (CCS)*, pages 3–16, 2016.

GKZ19.   Peter Gazi, Aggelos Kiayias, and Dionysis Zindros.   Proof-of-stake
           sidechains. In *IEEE Symposium on Security & Privacy*, 2019.

HB96.   J. Hawkinson and T. Bates. Guidelines for creation, selection, and registration
           of an Autonomous System (AS), March 1996.

Heo15.   Tejun Heo. Control Group v2, October 2015. https://www.kernel.org
           /doc/Documentation/cgroup-v2.txt.

Her18.   Maurice Herlihy. Atomic cross-chain swaps. In *Proceedings of the 2018 ACM
           Symposium on Principles of Distributed Computing*, pages 245–254. ACM, 2018.

HKD07.   Andreas Haeberlen, Petr Kouznetsov, and Peter Druschel. PeerReview: Prac-
           tical accountability for distributed systems. *SOSP*, 2007.

HKJR10.   Patrick Hunt, Mahadev Konar, Flavio P. Junqueira, and Benjamin Reed.
           Zookeeper: Wait-free coordination for internet-scale systems. In *ATC*, pages
           11–11. USENIX, 2010.

HKZG15.   Ethan Heilman, Alison Kendler, Aviv Zohar, and Sharon Goldberg. Eclipse
           attacks on bitcoin's peer-to-peer network. In *24th USENIX Security Sympo-
           sium*, pages 129–144, 2015.

HLS19.   Maurice Herlihy, Barbara Liskov, and Liuba Shrira. Cross-chain deals and
           adversarial commerce. *Proc. VLDB Endow.*, 13:100–113, October 2019.

HMW18.   Timo Hanke, Mahnush Movahedi, and Dominic Williams. DFINITY technol-
          ogy overview series, consensus system. Technical Report 1805.04548, arXiv,
          May 2018.
HRL06.   Susan Hares, Yakov Rekhter, and Tony Li. A Border Gateway Protocol 4
          (BGP-4), January 2006.
HSV+22.   David Hyland, Joao Sousa, Gauthier Voron, Alysson Bessani, and Vincent
          Gramoli. Ten myths about blockchain consensus. In *Blockchains - A Handbook
          on Fundamentals, Platforms and Applications*. Springer, 2022.
IBM75.   IBM. Data encryption standard, 1975.
IP.   IP Address to Identify Geolocation Information. http://www.ip2locat
          ion.com/.
IP2.   IP Address Details - ipinfo.io. http://ipinfo.io/.
IP3.   IP Address Geolocation to trace Country, Region, City, ZIP Code, etc. http
          s://www.eurekapi.com/.
IP4.   IP Geolocation and Online Fraud Prevention | MaxMind. https://www.
          maxmind.com/en/home.
KAD+07.   Ramakrishna Kotla, Lorenzo Alvisi, Mike Dahlin, Allen Clement, and Ed-
          mund Wong. Zyzzyva: Speculative byzantine fault tolerance. In *Proceedings
          of Twenty-first ACM SIGOPS Symposium on Operating Systems Principles*, SOSP
          '07, pages 45–58, New York, NY, USA, 2007. ACM.
KGF18.   Rami Khalil, Arthur Gervais, and Guillaume Felley. NOCUST–a securely
          scalable commit-chain. Technical Report 642, Cryptology ePrint Archive,
          2018.
KJG+16.   Eleftherios Kokoris Kogias, Philipp Jovanovic, Nicolas Gailly, Ismail Khoffi,
          Linus Gasser, and Bryan Ford. Enhancing bitcoin security and performance
          with strong consistency via collective signing. In *25th USENIX Security Sym-
          posium (USENIX Security 16)*, pages 279–296, Austin, TX, 2016. USENIX As-
          sociation.
KKJG+17a. Eleftherios Kokoris-Kogias, Philipp Jovanovic, Linus Gasser, Nicolas Gailly,
          Ewa Syta, and Bryan Ford. Omniledger: A secure, scale-out, decentralized
          ledger. Technical Report 2017/405, Cryptology ePrint, 2017.
KKJG+17b. Eleftherios Kokoris-Kogias, Philipp Jovanovic, Linus Gasser, Nicolas Gailly,
          Ewa Syta, and Bryan Ford. Omniledger: A secure, scale-out, decentralized
          ledger via sharding. Cryptology ePrint Archive, Report 2017/406, 2017. ht
          tps://eprint.iacr.org/2017/406.
KKJG+18. Eleftherios Kokoris-Kogias, Philipp Jovanovic, Linus Gasser, Nicolas Gailly,
          Ewa Syta, and Bryan Ford. Omniledger: A secure, scale-out, decentralized
          ledger via sharding. In *2018 IEEE Symposium on Security and Privacy (SP)*,
          pages 583–598, 2018.
KS16.   Valerie King and Jared Saia. Byzantine agreement in expected polynomial
          time. *J. ACM*, 63(2):13, 2016.
Lam11.   Leslie Lamport. Brief announcement: Leaderless byzantine paxos. In *Dis-
          tributed Computing - 25th International Symposium, DISC 2011, Rome, Italy,
          September 20-22, 2011. Proceedings*, pages 141–142, 2011.
LNE+18.   Joshua Lind, Oded Naor, Ittay Eyal, Florian Kelbert, Peter Pietzuch, and
          Emin Gün Sirer. Teechain: Reducing storage costs on the blockchain with
          offline payment channels. In *Proceedings of the 11th ACM International Sys-
          tems and Storage Conference*, pages 125–125. ACM, 2018.
LNZ+16.   Loi Luu, Viswesh Narayanan, Chaodong Zheng, Kunal Baweja, Seth Gilbert,
          and Prateek Saxena. A secure sharding protocol for open blockchains. In *Pro-
          ceedings of the 2016 ACM SIGSAC Conference on Computer and Communications
          Security*, CCS '16, pages 17–30, 2016.
LS14.   Pat Litke and Joe Stewart. BGP hijacking for cryptocurrency profit, August
          2014.

LSP82.   Leslie Lamport, Robert Shostak, and Marshall Pease. The byzantine generals problem. *ACM Trans. Program. Lang. Syst.*, 4(3):382–401, July 1982.

Lyn96.   Nancy A. Lynch. *Distributed Algorithms*. Morgan Kaufmann, 1996.

MBKM17.   Andrew Miller, Iddo Bentov, Ranjit Kumaresan, and Patrick McCorry. Sprites: Payment channels that go faster than lightning. Technical Report 1702.05812, arXiv, 2017.

Mer.   Merit RADb. http://www.radb.net/.

MJM09.   Yanhua Mao, Flavio P. Junqueira, and Keith Marzullo. Towards low latency state machine replication for uncivil wide-area networks. In *In Workshop on Hot Topics in System Dependability*, 2009.

MMR15a.   A. Mostéfaoui, H. Moumen, and M. Raynal. Signature-free asynchronous binary byzantine consensus with $t < n/3$, $o(n^2)$ messages, and $o(1)$ expected time. *Journal of ACM*, 62(4), 2015.

MMR15b.   Achour Mostéfaoui, Hamouma Moumen, and Michel Raynal. Signature-free asynchronous binary byzantine consensus with $T < N/3$, $O(N^2)$ messages, and $O(1)$ expected time. *J. ACM*, 62(4):31:1–31:21, September 2015.

Nak08.   Satoshi Nakamoto. Bitcoin: a peer-to-peer electronic cash system, 2008. http://www.bitcoin.org.

NBF$^+$16.   Arvind Narayanan, Joseph Bonneau, Edward Felten, Andrew Miller, and Steven Goldfeder. *Bitcoin and Cryptocurrency Technologies: A Comprehensive Introduction*. Princeton University Press, USA, 2016.

NCV05.   Nuno F. Neves, Miguel Correia, and Paulo Verissimo. Solving vector consensus with a wormhole. *IEEE Trans. Parallel Distrib. Syst.*, 16(12):1120–1131, December 2005.

NG16a.   Christopher Natoli and Vincent Gramoli. The balance attack against proof-of-work blockchains: The R3 testbed as an example. Technical Report 1765133, arXiv, 2016.

NG16b.   Christopher Natoli and Vincent Gramoli. The blockchain anomaly. In *Proceedings of the 15th IEEE International Symposium on Network Computing and Applications (NCA'16)*, pages 310–317, Oct 2016.

NG17.   Christopher Natoli and Vincent Gramoli. The balance attack or why forkable blockchains are ill-suited for consortium. In *Proceedings of the 47th IEEE/IFIP International Conference on Dependable Systems and Networks (DSN'17)*, June 2017.

NKMS16.   Kartik Nayak, Srijan Kumar, Andrew Miller, and Elaine Shi. Stubborn mining: Generalizing selfish mining and combining with an eclipse attack. In *IEEE European Symposium on Security and Privacy, EuroS&P 2016, Saarbrücken, Germany, March 21-24, 2016*, pages 305–320, 2016.

Nol16.   Tier Nolan. Atomic swaps using cut and choose. https://bitcointalk.org/index.php?topic=1364951, 2016.

NYGEV19. Christopher Natoli, Jiangshan Yu, Vincent Gramoli, and Paulo Esteves-Verissimo. Deconstructing blockchains: A comprehensive survey on consensus, membership and structure. Technical Report 1908.08316, arXiv, 2019.

PB17.   Joseph Poon and Vitalik Buterin. Plasma: Scalable autonomous smart contracts. *White paper*, pages 1–47, 2017.

PD16.   Joseph Poon and Thaddeus Dryja. The bitcoin lightning network: Scalable off-chain instant payments, 2016.

Pro20.   Bitcoin Project. Some things you need to know, 2020. https://bitcoin.org/en/you-need-to-know.

PSL80.   M. Pease, R. Shostak, and L. Lamport. Reaching agreement in the presence of faults. *J. ACM*, 27(2):228–234, April 1980.

PSS16.   Rafael Pass, Lior Seeman, and Abhi Shelat. Analysis of the blockchain protocol in asynchronous networks. Technical Report 454, Crytology ePrint Archive, 2016.

Rab83.   Michael O. Rabin. Randomized byzantine generals. In *Proceedings of the 24th Annual Symposium on Foundations of Computer Science*, SFCS '83, pages 403–409, 1983.

Ray10.   Michel Raynal. *Communication and Agreement Abstractions for Fault-Tolerant Asynchronous Distributed Systems*. Morgan and Claypool Publishers, 1st edition, 2010.

Ray18.   Michel Raynal. *Fault-Tolerant Message-Passing Distributed Systems - An Algorithmic Approach*. Springer, 2018.

RG22.   Alejandro Ranchal-Pedrosa and Vincent Gramoli. TRAP: the bait of rational players to solve byzantine consensus. In Yuji Suga, Kouichi Sakurai, Xuhua Ding, and Kazue Sako, editors, *Proceedings of the ACM Asia Conference on Computer and Communications Security (Asia CCS'22)*, pages 168–181. ACM, 2022.

Roc18.   Team Rocket. Snowflake to avalanche: A novel metastable consensus protocol family for cryptocurrencies, 2018. Unpublished manuscript.

Ros12.   Meni Rosenfeld. Analysis of hashrate-based double-spending, 2012.

RPG19.   Alejandro Ranchal-Pedrosa and Vincent Gramoli. Platypus: Offchain protocol without synchrony. In *Proceedings of the 18th IEEE International Symposium on Network Computing and Applications (NCA'19)*, pages 1–8. IEEE, Sep 2019.

RPG20.   Alejandro Ranchal-Pedrosa and Vincent Gramoli. Blockchain is dead, long live blockchain! Accountable state machine replication for longlasting blockchain. Technical Report 2007.10541, arXiv, 2020.

SBV18.   Joao Sousa, Alysson Bessani, and Marko Vukolić. A byzantine fault-tolerant ordering service for the hyperledger fabric blockchain platform. In *2018 48th Annual IEEE/IFIP International Conference on Dependable Systems and Networks (DSN)*, pages 51–58, June 2018.

Shi.   Elaine Shi. Foundations of distributed consensus and blockchains (preliminary draft). Retrieved online on 29 Sept. 2020.

SNG20.   Gary Shapiro, Christopher Natoli, and Vincent Gramoli. The performance of Byzantine fault tolerant blockchains. In *Proceedings of the 19th IEEE International Symposium on Network Computing and Applications (NCA'20)*. IEEE, Nov 2020.

SWN⁺21.   Peiyao Sheng, Gerui Wang, Kartik Nayak, Sreeram Kannan, and Pramod Viswanath. Bft protocol forensics. In *Computer and Communication Security (CCS)*, Nov 2021.

SZ15.   Yonatan Sompolinsky and Aviv Zohar. Secure high-rate transaction processing in bitcoin. In *Financial Cryptography and Data Security - 19th International Conference, FC 2015, San Juan, Puerto Rico, January 26-30, 2015, Revised Selected Papers*, pages 507–527, 2015.

Sza97.   Nick Szabo. Formalizing and securing relationships on public networks, 1997. http://szabo.best.vwh.net/formalize.html.

Sza05.   Nick Szabo. Bit gold, 2005.

TG19.   Pierre Tholoniat and Vincent Gramoli. Formal verification of blockchain Byzantine fault tolerance. In *6th Workshop on Formal Reasoning in Distributed Algorithms (FRIDA'19)*, Oct 2019.

TG22.   Pierre Tholoniat and Vincent Gramoli. Formal verification of blockchain byzantine fault tolerance. In *Handbook on Blockchain*. Springer Nature, 2022.

THG22.   Deepal Tennakoon, Yiding Hua, and Vincent Gramoli. CollaChain: A BFT collaborative middleware for decentralized applications. Technical Report 2203.12323, arXiv, 2022.

TTK22.   *Handbook on Blockchain*. Springer Nature, 2022. To appear 2022.

VCB⁺09.   Giuliana Veronese, Miguel Correia, Alysson Bessani, Lau Cheuk Lung, and Paulo Verissimo. Minimal byzantine fault tolerance. Technical Report TR-2009-15, DI-FCUL, June 2009.

vec11.   vector76. The vector76 attack, August 2011.

VG19a.   Guillaume Vizier and Vincent Gramoli. Comchain: A blockchain with Byzantine fault tolerant reconfiguration. *Concurrency and Computation, Practice and Experience*, 32(12), Oct 2019.

VG19b.   Gauthier Voron and Vincent Gramoli. Dispel: Byzantine SMR with distributed pipelining. Technical Report 1912.10367, arXiv, 2019.

vGGT20.   Rob van Glabbeek, Vincent Gramoli, and Pierre Tholoniat. Feasibility of cross-chain payment with success guarantees. In *Proceedings of the 32nd ACM Symposium on Parallelism in Algorithms and Architectures*, page 579?581, 2020.

Vuk16.   Marco Vukolíc. The quest for scalable blockchain fabric: Proof-of-work vs. BFT replication. In *Proceedings of the IFIP WG 11.4 Workshop on Open Research Problems in Network Security (iNetSec 2015)*, LNCS, pages 112–125, 2016.

Wat16.   Roger Wattenhofer. *The Science of the Blockchain*. CreateSpace Independent Publishing Platform, North Charleston, SC, USA, 1st edition, 2016.

Woo15.   Gavin Wood. Ethereum: A secure decentralised generalised transaction ledger, 2015. Yellow paper.

WW19.   Jiaping Wang and Hao Wang. Monoxide: Scale out blockchains with asynchronous consensus zones. In *16th USENIX Symposium on Networked Systems Design and Implementation (NSDI 19)*, pages 95–112, Boston, MA, February 2019. USENIX Association.

XPZ+16.   Xiwei Xu, Cesare Pautasso, Liming Zhu, Vincent Gramoli, Alexander Ponomarev, An Binh Tran, and Shiping Chen. The blockchain as a software connector. In *13th Working IEEE/IFIP Conference on Software Architecture, WICSA 2016, Venice, Italy, April 5-8, 2016*, pages 182–191, 2016.

XWS19.   Xiwei Xu, Ingo Weber, and Mark Staples. *Architecture for Blockchain Applications*. Springer, 1st edition, 2019.

YKDE19.   J. Yu, D. Kozhaya, J. Decouchant, and P. Esteves-Verissimo. Repucoin: Your reputation is your power. *IEEE Transactions on Computers*, 68(8):1225–1237, 2019.

YMR+19.   Maofan Yin, Dahlia Malkhi, Michael K. Reiter, Guy Golan-Gueta, and Ittai Abraham. HotStuff: BFT consensus with linearity and responsiveness. In *Proceedings of the 2019 ACM Symposium on Principles of Distributed Computing*, pages 347–356, 2019.

ZAA19.   Victor Zakhary, Divyakant Agrawal, and Amr El Abbadi. Atomic commitment across blockchains. Technical Report 1905.02847, arXiv, 2019.

ZHL+18.   Alexei Zamyatin, Dominik Harz, Joshua Lind, Panayiotis Panayiotou, Arthur Gervais, and William J Knottenbelt. Xclaim: Interoperability with cryptocurrency-backed tokens. Technical Report 2018/643, Cryptology ePrint Archive, 2018.

ZMR18.   Mahdi Zamani, Mahnush Movahedi, and Mariana Raykova. Rapidchain: Scaling blockchain via full sharding. Cryptology ePrint Archive, Report 2018/460, 2018. https://eprint.iacr.org/2018/460.

Chapter 8
Glossary

address   the identifier of an account. 10

AS   a set of Internet Protocol prefixes belonging to networks that are all managed by a single entity. 62

BBC   Binary Byzantine Consensus. 87

BC   Byzantine Consensus. 47

blockchain   a chain of blocks that initially starts with a genesis block where each new block points to the last appended block. 7

Byzantine   denotes a node that can fail in an arbitrary manner. 18

conflict   two concurrently issued transactions try to withdraw from the same account the same assets. 9

consensus   a distributed computing problem that consists of ensuring no two nodes decide different values (agreement), that the decided value is one of the proposed value (validity) and that eventually every correct node decides (termination). 3, 12

crash   denotes a failure where a node halts. 19

DAG   Directed Acyclic Graph. 8

DAO   Decentralized Autonomous Organisation. 7

double-spending   denotes the result of spending the same assets twice. 10

fork   a set of multiple pointers pointing to the same block in a blockchain. 11

Geth   the version of the Ethereum protocol written in the Go programming language. 2

GST   Global Stabilization Time. 23

LAN   Local Area Network. 82, 83

leader-based   denotes a consensus algorithm where a unique particular node, the leader, sends its proposal to collect enough votes on this proposal. 81

© Springer Nature Switzerland AG 2022
V. Gramoli, *Blockchain Scalability and its Foundations in Distributed Systems*,
https://doi.org/10.1007/978-3-031-12578-2

leaderless   denotes a consensus algorithm that is not leader-based. 81

mining   the action of trying to combine transactions into a new block. 10
mining power   the computational power of a miner. 24

partially synchronous communication   an assumption under which every
    message gets delivered within an unknown period of time. 23
proof-of-work   the solution to a cryptopuzzle that is computationally hard
    to find but easy to verify.. 3, 6, 7

scalability   the ability for a system to preserve or improve its properties as
    it grows. 80
set   a set of objects $v_1, ..., v_k$ is denoted $\{v_1, ..., v_k\}$. 10
smart contract   programs that can be invoked by other users and executed
    on the blockchain. 7
superblock   a block decided by a Set Byzantine Consensus algorithm and
    that results from the combination of the individual batches of transactions
    proposed by distinct nodes. 85
synchronous communication   an assumption under which every message
    gets delivered within a known period of time. 22

transaction   a transfer of digital assets or coins from a source account to a
    destination account. 10
tuple   a tuple of objects $v_1, ..., v_k$ is denoted $\langle v_1, ..., v_k \rangle$; a tuple of two objects
    v_1, v_2 is called a pair. 9

UTXO   Unspent Transaction Output. 9, 13

WAN   Wide Area Network. 83

Printed in the United States
by Baker & Taylor Publisher Services